C0-DAM-810

Witnesses of
THE
BIRTH OF
CHRIST

Witnesses of THE BIRTH OF CHRIST

JOSEPH FIELDING McCONKIE

Illustrated by Vivian McConkie Adams

Bookcraft
Salt Lake City, Utah

Copyright © 1998 by Bookcraft, Inc.

All rights reserved. No part of this book may be repro-
duced in any form or by any means without permission in
writing from the publisher, Bookcraft, Inc., 2405 W.
Orton Circle, West Valley City, Utah 84119.

Bookcraft is a registered trademark of Bookcraft, Inc.

Library of Congress Catalog Card Number 98-74084
ISBN 1-57008-578-1

First Printing, 1998

Printed in the United States of America

Contents

Preface

No story in the Christian world is more loved than that of the birth of Christ. It is a story to be told and retold. It has been depicted more often in art, heralded more frequently in hymn, spoken of more consistently in churches, and enacted more repeatedly in pageants than any other Bible story. The irony that attends such devotion is the near-universal misunderstanding of the real meaning of the story, not to mention how commonly it is mistold. Admittedly, the manner in which the story has been preserved for us allows, even requires, some interpretive commentary. Done properly, this but adds to our feelings of reverence and respect. Still we need not expect any two commentaries to be in perfect agreement. No scene catches everyone's eye as exactly the same. The point of universal agreement for Latter-day Saints is that the child born of Mary in the stable at Bethlehem was in very deed the Son of God.

Nor should it go unobserved that as we grow in understanding of the events that surrounded the birth of our Savior, we will also grow in love and reverence for him and in our knowledge of the nature and significance of his earthly ministry. For these reasons, but primarily because I too love the story, I thought this small volume might be appropriate.

In writing it I have drawn freely on the revelations of the Restoration and the writings of modern prophets. The light that comes from these sources enables us to see and understand much that would otherwise be lost to us. I have also sought to acquaint myself with the best of what the scholars of the world have had to say, both those who write with faith and those who do not. Suffice it to say that much that has been written about this story carries no light with it, and it simply doesn't taste good.

In all of this we can be certain it was never intended that the birth of God's Son be kept secret. It was first announced to Adam and Eve and has been known to all the holy prophets since the world began. It was heralded by angels to men and women, to the old and the young, to the great and the small alike.

We fondly look for that great day when all will have heard the testimony of his divine sonship and, having heard, believe; and believing, rejoice. To him we bow the knee; for he alone is our King.

Prologue:
At the Peril of
Our Salvation

We accept or reject Jesus of Nazareth's claim to divine sonship at the peril of our eternal lives. If he is God's Son, salvation is found in him and in no other. If he is not the Son of God, then, as Paul phrased it, our preaching is vain and our faith also (see 1 Corinthians 15:14).

Christ's claim to divine sonship is the hinge upon which the door of salvation swings. Without the unique inheritance that was his by birth—that is, the power to lay down his life, which he inherited from his mother, Mary, and the ability to take it up again, which he inherited from his Father, who is God—there could have been no atonement. Without the Atonement all else is lost. Thus only in Christ is the power found to rectify the effects of Adam's fall.

As the effects of the Fall were universal, so were the effects of the Atonement. "As in Adam all die, even so in Christ shall all be made alive" (1 Corinthians 15:22). In so saying we have in mind not just the inseparable union of body and spirit in what we call resurrection, but also the reconciliation of the immortal soul with the heavenly family from which it came. In order for this to take place all people must have the fulness of the gospel preached to them, that they may have the opportunity to embrace its truths and comply with its ordinances. Those not granted the privilege to hear these truths in this life must have that opportunity in the world of spirits before the time of resurrection and the day of judgment.

The evidence that salvation comes through Christ must be sufficiently clear and credible that all who are guided by the light of the Spirit can with certainty know of the verity of Christ's divine sonship. If the story of his birth could be impeached, we could justifiably be excused from accepting it. We would then be without obligation to Christ and his gospel. It would be our right, even our duty, to direct the hope of our salvation elsewhere.

That, however, is not the case. This book seeks to bring to you, the reader, the compelling testimony of the witnesses of Christ's birth as we have them from both the Old World and the New World, from revelation both ancient and modern, that you might be a confident and competent witness of his birth and his divine sonship.

The Birth of Christ
As Announced in the Old World

The story is most remarkable. In it we find the testimony of heaven and earth combining as a marvelous choir heralds the birth of God's Son. The story begins with the declaration of a messenger from God's presence to Zacharias, who was the rightful heir of Aaron's seat (though he had been denied it), to prepare the way before the Savior. We find this son of Aaron standing before the altar of the temple clothed in the robes of the priesthood, as his prayer ascends with those of his nation asking for the fulfillment of the long-sought promise of their Messiah's coming. So it is that the angel also declares the birth of Christ to a young virgin in the despised village of Nazareth in Galilee and takes these tidings also to the man to whom she is betrothed, and yet who will not be the father of her son.

Attendant to these events, he whom we know as John the Baptist, while yet in his mother's womb, leaped for joy in recognition of the mother of the Christ child, while his own mother, for whom childbirth was supposed to be impossible, rejoiced in song and testimony with Mary. Then a chorus of angels declared the birth of Christ to humble shepherds tending their sheep in the fields, who were told that they would find the child lying in a cattle trough. In the temple the aged Simeon awaited the time when he would take the Son of the Highest in his arms and the widow Anna would rejoice and spread the good news. Thereafter came the wise men from afar, who announced the Messiah's birth to Herod, Israel's illegitimate king, and then paid their own homage to the rightful heir of Israel's throne. Thus the small and the great, male and female, young and old combined their voices to herald the birth of the Son of God.

The paradox of his birth would yet be reflected in the paradox of his ministry. Edersheim describes it thus: "If He was born of the humble Maiden of Nazareth, an Angel announced His birth; if the Infant-Saviour was cradled in a manger, the shining host of heaven hymned His Advent. And so afterwards—if He hungered and was tempted in the wilderness, Angels ministered to Him, even as an Angel strengthened Him in the agony of the garden. If He submitted to baptism, the Voice and vision from heaven attested His Sonship; if enemies threatened, He could miraculously pass through them; if the Jews assailed, there was the Voice of God to glorify Him; if He was nailed to the cross, the sun craped his brightness, and earth quaked; if He was laid in the tomb, Angels kept its watches, and heralded His rising. And so, when now the Mother of Jesus, in her humbleness, could only bring the 'poor's offering,' the witness to the greatness of Him Whom she had borne was not wanting." (Alfred Edersheim, *The Life and Times of Jesus the Messiah,* Hendrickson, 1993, p. 138.)

The Birth of Christ
As Announced in the New World

There is but one gospel of salvation and one Savior for all the inhabitants of the earth. The knowledge of his coming is of equal importance to all, whether they live in great cities or in isolated hamlets; whether they live upon the great trade routes or in some forgotten place; be it in the Old World or the New. If they be Adam's seed and thus know of death and pain, of sorrow and sin, they must come to know of the birth of God's Son. The faithful, wherever they be, have equal claim upon the revelations of heaven. If prophets herald his birth in the Old World, their New World counterparts must bear the same testimony; if angels visit those prepared to receive them among one people, so it must be among all such people; if signs in the heavens be given one nation they must be given to all nations. The Book of Mormon attests that such was the case in the Western Hemisphere and also assures us that we will yet receive the records of the other transplanted remnants of Israel, from which we will learn that they too knew of these singular truths.

As to the prophecies of Christ's birth and earthly ministry that were known among the Nephites, we will yet see that they differed from those of the Old World only in that they were more explicit. With that knowledge came a greater degree of accountability, as witnessed by the destruction that took place in the Americas at the time of his death. Whereas some among the faithful in the Old World were aware of a new star announcing the night of his birth, in the New World "at the going down of the sun there was no darkness," and throughout the land all saw the star announcing his birth. (See 3 Nephi 1:14–17.) While those among whom he had preached experienced three hours of darkness (from noon till three), those in the New World, along with all other scattered remnants of Israel, would experience three days of darkness at the time of his death (see Matthew 27:45; 1 Nephi 19:10; Helaman 14:20).

Such were left without excuse because of the plainness of the prophecy that was known among them. Samuel the Lamanite had prophesied that there would be no darkness during the night of the Savior's birth, and the promised sign had now been seen by all. "And it came to pass also that a new star did appear, according to the word. And it came to pass that from this time forth there began to be lyings sent forth among the people, by Satan, to harden their hearts, to the intent that they might not believe in those signs and wonders which they had seen; but notwithstanding these lyings and deceivings the more part of the people did believe, and were converted unto the Lord." (3 Nephi 1:21–22.) The whole face of the land was changed by the destructions visited upon those who had rejected and killed the prophets who had testified of these things.

The Testimony of Our Dispensation

The testimony that we as Latter-day Saints have been commissioned to bear in all the world is that the heavens have again been opened, that the God of heaven speaks to us as he did to the ancients, and that a new gospel dispensation has been introduced. A gospel dispensation is a period of time in which all saving truths are restored or revealed anew from heaven so that the believers' knowledge of the saving principles of the gospel stands independent of those of the past. Thus if Jesus of Nazareth is indeed God's Son, modern revelation must so attest with sufficient certainty that we need not be beholden to the faith of other people in other times. Though we rejoice in their testimony and are enriched by it, our testimony stands independent of it.

The dawn of the Restoration occurred in upstate New York on a spring morning in the year 1820. In a secluded grove near the township of Palmyra the youthful Joseph Smith sought the direction of heaven to know which of all the churches he should join. In response to his humble prayer a magnificent light, one that shone above the brightness of the noonday sun, descended from the heavens. In the midst of that light he saw two Personages who, he said, exactly resembled each other in features and likeness. One of them addressed him saying: "Joseph, this is my Beloved Son. Hear him." (Joseph Smith—History 1:17).

Much that is of immeasurable worth was spoken that day. For our purposes, however, it is sufficient to observe that the first sentence spoken by the God of heaven in this the greatest of all gospel dispensations attested to the divine sonship of Jesus

Christ. From that moment to this, the "Beloved Son" has been the source of every revelation and truth espoused by the Latter-day Saints.

In the revelations of the Restoration Christ has repeatedly testified of himself and his relationship with the Father. Nearly a year before the Church was organized, in a revelation given to David Whitmer, there came these words: "Behold, I am Jesus Christ, the Son of the living God, who created the heavens and the earth, a light which cannot be hid in darkness" (D&C 14:9). Teaching the doctrine of unity and oneness, a revelation addressed to Joseph Smith and Sidney Rigdon stated: "I am Jesus Christ, the Son of God, who was crucified for the sins of the world, even as many as will believe on my name, that they may become the sons of God, even one in me as I am one in the Father, as the Father is one in me, that we may be one" (D&C 35:2). In a revelation designated as the law of the Church, we are told again that Jesus Christ is "the Son of the Living God, the Savior of the world" and that we must heed his word (D&C 42:1–2).

To the missionaries going forth to declare the message of the Restoration he said: "Wherefore, be of good cheer, and do not fear, for I the Lord am with you, and will stand by you; and ye shall bear record of me, even Jesus Christ, that I am the Son of the living God, that I was, that I am, and that I am to come" (D&C 68:6). To all parents in the Church he said: "And again, inasmuch as parents have children in Zion, or in any of her stakes which are organized, that teach them not to understand the doctrine of repentance, faith in Christ the Son of the living God, and of baptism and the gift of the Holy Ghost by the laying on of the hands, when eight years old, the sin be upon the heads of the parents" (D&C 68:25). And in the revelation on the subject of the degrees of glory a vision was opened to Joseph Smith and Sidney Rigdon of which they testified saying: "For we saw him, even on the right hand of God; and we heard the voice bearing record that he is the Only Begotten of the Father—that by him, and through him, and of him, the worlds are and were created, and the inhabitants thereof are begotten sons and daughters unto God" (D&C 76:23–24). Indeed, the frequency with which Christ testified of his divine sonship might well be taken as a mandate that we do likewise.

The Testimony of Scripture

It is significant that we have been blessed with the knowledge and testimony of scriptural records relative to the birth of Christ that come from three distinct dispensations: the meridian dispensation as found in the New Testament, the New World as found in the Book of Mormon, and our own day as found in the revelations of the Restoration. Thus we have the doctrine of Christ's divine sonship established for us in the mouth of three witnesses. No other generation has been better prepared to testify of this supernal event than our own.

CHAPTER ONE

New Witnesses of the Divine Sonship of Christ

In a vision Nephi beheld the city of Nazareth

Latter-day Saints our understanding of the divine sonship of Christ is not confined to the writings of Matthew and Luke. Through the revelations of the Restoration all saving doctrines have been revealed anew. In addition to the revelations of the Restoration we have had ancient records restored to us from which we also obtain a flood of knowledge as to the faith and understanding of the ancient Saints. The story of the birth of Christ and its true doctrinal significance constitutes a wonderful illustration of what we have been given. Indeed, our testimony of this most sacred event combines the testimony of three gospel dispensations: that of the New Testament, the testimony of Book of Mormon prophets, and the revelations of the Restoration as given through the Prophet Joseph Smith.

As noted in the prologue, a gospel dispensation is a period of time in which the doctrines of salvation are dispensed or given anew from the heavens in sufficient measure that those to whom they are given are not beholden to any other people for their knowledge of the plan of salvation. Certainly this was the case with those with whom Christ ministered in the land of Palestine. Until the death of the Apostles they had sufficient knowledge of the gospel and priesthood power to perform the ordinances of salvation. From the Book of Mormon we learn that the same authority and doctrines were operative in the Americas.

Once again, in our day the saving principles of the gospel and the priesthood have been restored along with the testimony of those who have lived in ages past. In this gathering of scriptural records, which is a part of the dispensation of the fulness of times, we find that the sum of the parts becomes greater than the whole; that is, the testimony of the past and that of the present enhance and enrich each other. In their union comes an understanding that cannot otherwise be had.

This is simply an expression of the law of witnesses. One provision of this law holds that no testimony of divine truth is required to stand alone; rather, all that comes from heaven will be evidenced by two or more witnesses. Not only do the separate witnesses collaborate each other but they also expand, extend, and enhance each other. So it is that the testimonies relative to the birth of Christ, as they have been preserved for us in the Bible, the Book of Mormon, and the Doctrine and Covenants, join together to fortify and enrich our understanding of the doctrine of the divine sonship of Christ.

The Bible and the Law of Witnesses

From the Bible we learn that in ancient Israel the testimony of one man was not sufficient to convict another of sin (see Deuteronomy 17:6; 19:15). Christ expanded this principle, directing that "if thy brother shall trespass against thee, go and tell him his fault between thee and him alone: if he shall hear thee, thou hast gained thy brother. But if he will not hear thee, then take with thee one or two more, that in the mouth of two or three witnesses every word may be established." (Matthew 18:15–16.) Bible commentators, however, have not seen any relationship between this law and the teaching of the gospel. That the law does apply to the teaching of the gospel, however, is evident from the Pharisees' challenge to the Master and the latter's response. "Thou bearest record of thy self; thy record is not true," they charged. "I am not alone," Christ countered. "It is also written in your law that the testimony of two men is true. I am one that bear witness of myself, and the Father that sent me beareth witness of me." (John 8:13, 16–18.) Clearly the law required two people as witnesses to establish a gospel principle, as it did to establish the truth in all other matters.

Perhaps the reason why writers of other faiths avoid commentary on these verses involves the clear distinction the scriptures make between the Father and the Son and Christ's assertion that his Father was indeed in the form of a man. Be that as it may, it is certain that the nation of the Jews knew well that "the Lord always sends his word by witnesses who testify of its truth and divinity; that one witness alone, though he speaks the truth, is not enough to bind his hearers; that two or more witnesses always unite their voices to make the divinely borne testimony binding on earth and sealed everlastingly in the heavens; and that, thus, in the mouth of two or three witnesses every word shall be established." (Bruce R. McConkie, *The Mortal Messiah*, Salt Lake City: Deseret Book Co., 1980, 2:76.)

The Law of Witnesses in the Book of Mormon

That the teaching of the gospel was to comply with the law of witnesses is plainly taught in the Book of Mormon. We have no reason to suppose that Lehi and his family did not know this principle before they left the Old World. From their writings we learn that the gospel was to be taught by authorized witnesses to those of every nation, kindred, tongue, and people. Further, that no man's testimony was to stand alone, but that in the testimony of two or three men all things would be established. So it is that Nephi tells us: "By the words of three, God hath said, I will establish my word. Nevertheless, God sendeth more witnesses, and he proveth all his words." (2 Nephi 11:3.)

With an understanding of the law of witnesses and with the foreknowledge of how his testimony and that of the other prophets of the New World would be received, Nephi wrote:

Many of the Gentiles shall say: A Bible! A Bible! We have got a Bible, and there cannot be any more Bible.

But thus saith the Lord God: O fools, they shall have a Bible; and it shall proceed forth from the Jews, mine ancient covenant people. And what thank they the Jews for the Bible which they receive from them? . . . .

Thou fool, that shall say: A Bible, we have got a Bible, and we need no more Bible. Have ye obtained a Bible save it were by the Jews?

Know ye not that there are more nations than one? Know ye not that I, the Lord your God, have created all men, and that I remember those who are upon the isles of the sea; and that I rule in the heavens above and in the earth beneath; and I bring forth my word unto the children of men, yea, even upon all the nations of the earth?

Wherefore murmur ye, because that ye shall receive more of my word? Know ye not that the testimony of two nations is a witness unto you that I am God, that I remember one nation like unto another? Wherefore, I speak the same words unto one nation like unto another. And when the two nations shall run together the testimony of the two nations shall run together also.

And I do this that I may prove unto many that I am the same yesterday, today, and forever; and that I speak forth my words according to mine own pleasure. And because that I have spoken one word ye need not suppose that I cannot speak another; for my work is not yet finished; neither shall it be until the end of man, neither from that time henceforth and forever.

Wherefore, because that ye have a Bible ye need not suppose that it contains all my words; neither need ye suppose that I have not caused more to be written. (2 Nephi 29:3–10.)

Our Dispensation and the Law of Witnesses

It was in compliance with the law of witnesses that Christ sent his disciples out to declare the message of the gospel two by two (see Mark 6:7; Luke 10:1). In the revelation known as "the law" or the "law of the Church" that same system was restored in our day. "And ye shall go forth in the power of my Spirit, preaching my gospel, two by two, in my name, lifting up your voices as with the sound of a trump, declaring my word like unto angels of God" (D&C 42:6). Commenting on this principle, Elder B. H. Roberts explained: "It is the law of the Gospel that the Elders should travel two by two, mainly for the reason, I suppose, that God has declared that He would establish his word in the mouth of two or three witnesses; and it is good when bearing testimony to the world that there should be the legal number of witnesses provided for in the law of God." (Conference Report, October 1903, p. 76.) This same revelation also required that those who went forth be properly ordained, that they teach by the power of the Spirit, and that they teach from the scriptures (see D&C 42:6, 11–12). It is by these principles that we are to distinguish the authorized representatives or witnesses of the gospel from those who are without authority.

Written testimony, like its oral counterpart, requires a second witness to sustain its divine origin. It can be argued that this is accomplished by the testimony of the four Gospel writers in concert with the other books of the New Testament. To such an argument we have no objection. Surely this is a manifestation of the divine law. Yet would any honest-hearted soul feel to "murmur" because the testimony of still others was also made manifest to him? In the wisdom of the Lord he ordained yet another compilation of prophetic writings to come forth, one which stood entirely independent of the writings of the Old World. Such a record assures us of God's interest in all peoples and all nations. Further, such a record also stands as a point of reference in interpreting that which was written earlier. As the testimony of the two books becomes one a strait and sure course is established, thus protecting us from uninspired and self-serving interpretations.

Living Witnesses

That we not be tossed about with every wind of doctrine, it was ordained even in the councils of heaven that all gospel truths have the same source. That source is the priesthood. Joseph Smith taught the principle thus: The Melchizedek Priesthood, he said, "is the channel through which all knowledge, doctrine, the plan of salvation and every important matter is revealed from heaven" (*Teachings of the Prophet Joseph Smith,* Joseph Fielding Smith, comp., Salt Lake City: Deseret Book Co., 1976, pp. 166–67; hereafter cited as *Teachings.*) It is not enough that we have scriptural accounts of things. Devils can quote scripture as readily as prophets can. We must also have the Spirit and the authority by which the scriptures were originally given if we are to be in a position to properly understand them.

In the providence of God it was not intended that the Bible, the Book of Mormon, or the Doctrine and Covenants stand alone. For the testimony to be binding the doctrine of each must be declared by a legal administrator. "There is no salvation between the two lids of the Bible without a legal administrator," the Prophet said. "Jesus was then the legal administrator, and ordained His Apostles." (*Teachings,* p. 319.) That is to say that the "priesthood administereth the gospel," and thus the gospel—meaning each of its principles and ordinances—does not and cannot stand independent of the priesthood (D&C 84:19). Taking the nativity story as our example, whether it be taken from the Bible or the Book of Mormon, it must be sustained by the same Spirit and declared by the same authority in our day that it was anciently in order to have the same validity that it did anciently. The message cannot stand independent of the channel from which it comes.

To illustrate the principle let us suppose that in reading the Bible someone learns that the Savior said that unless a man is born of water and the Spirit he cannot enter the kingdom of heaven. Let us further suppose that this person then begins to declare the importance of baptism and even to "baptize" others.

Though there is a correctness in what he is doing, it is without authority. He has not been properly baptized, nor has he been commissioned to baptize others. Thus his witness about baptism, though well intended, is without the power of salvation. In like manner, the right to declare any doctrine, though it may not involve an ordinance, lacks the saving power that comes only from being properly commissioned to testify of it. Without that power one has not complied with the eternal law of witnesses.

The Testimony of the Book of Mormon

An understanding that God is a personal being, an exalted man, the father of our spirits, and the literal father of Christ in the flesh is essential to an understanding of the plan of salvation. None of these doctrines has been preserved in the Bible in such a manner that the Bible-believing world has been able to find and understand them. Yet standing in the light of heaven, Joseph Smith was able to take up the Bible and prove them all. Well might we liken the Bible to an unpolished diamond in a dimly lit room. Though many innately sense its immense worth, few imagine the splendor it will reveal once polished by the hands of those possessing the spirit of revelation and once it can be seen by the light of the restored gospel. This light makes the truths restored in our day so obvious to Latter-day Saint readers that they assume the Bible speaks with the same clarity to those of other faiths, forgetting that for them to see the same things they must be standing in the same light. Let us then lay the foundation of our understanding as the Prophet laid his; in a thoughtful study of the Book of Mormon and its testimony of the doctrine of divine sonship.

What then is it that we learn from the testimony of the prophets of the New World relative to the birth of Christ? By reading the Book of Mormon we learn that its peoples knew that God himself—that is, Jehovah, or the God of Abraham, Isaac, and Jacob—was to come to earth and take upon himself a tabernacle of flesh. They knew that the Old World would be the place of his birth and mortal ministry. They knew both the year and the day of his birth and the time of his death. His birth was announced to many by angels and was affirmed by signs in the heavens and the appearance of a new star. It was known that he was to be born of a virgin named Mary from the city of Nazareth, though the birth would take place "at [meaning, near] Jerusalem." They knew that he would be the Son of the Eternal Father, that his given name would be Jesus, and that he would bear the title Christ. Both the Messianic prophecies had by those in the New World and the doctrinal understanding that grows out of them far exceed those found in the Bible.

God to Come Down Among the Children of Men

The prophecies relative to the birth of Christ known to those who lived in the New World are appreciably more explicit and detailed than the prophecies preserved for us in the Old Testament. Among the Nephites it was clearly understood that Christ, as Redeemer of the world, was the God of the Old Testament and that he would come to earth and take upon himself a tabernacle of flesh. For instance, Abinadi testified to the wicked priests of King Noah saying:

> For behold, did not Moses prophesy unto them [the children of Israel] concerning the coming of the Messiah, and that God should redeem his people? Yea, and even all the prophets who have prophesied ever since the world began— have they not spoken more or less concerning these things?
>
> Have they not said that God himself should come down among the children of men, and take upon him the form of man, and go forth in mighty power upon the face of the earth?
>
> Yea, and have they not said also that he should bring to pass the resurrection of the dead, and that he, himself, should be oppressed and afflicted? (Mosiah 13:33–35.)

In bearing this testimony Abinadi affirmed that from the days of Adam "all the prophets who have prophesied" knew that "God himself should come down among the children of men, and take upon him the form of man." It was for this very testimony that he was put to death (see Mosiah 7:28). Abinadi, in concert with the other prophets of the Book of Mormon, correctly understood that salvation came in and through Christ; that he was their God and their Redeemer. They knew that salvation came in and through him and none else. Thus the testimony that Abinadi bore to the wicked priests of Noah's court was that "Christ was the God, the Father of all things [meaning Redeemer], and said that he should take upon him the image of man, and it should be the image after which man was created in the beginning; or in other words, he said that man was created after the image of God, and that God should come down among the children of men, and take upon him flesh and blood, and go forth upon the face of the earth" (Mosiah 7:27).

The breadth of Abinadi's understanding was such that his testimony of the sonship of Christ challenges the understanding of most readers of the Book of Mormon. "God himself shall come down among the children of men, and shall redeem his people," he said. Thus it was that Christ, the God of Abraham, Isaac, and Jacob, in order to work out an atoning sacrifice that all who so choose might have claim upon the blessings of salvation, came to the earth and took upon him a tabernacle of flesh. Abinadi continued:

> *And because he dwelleth in flesh he shall be called the Son of God, and having subjected the flesh to the will of the Father, being the Father and the Son—*
>
> *The Father, because he was conceived by the power of God; and the Son, because of the flesh; thus becoming the Father and Son—*
>
> *And they are one God, yea, the very Eternal Father of heaven and of earth.*
>
> *And thus the flesh becoming subject to the Spirit, or the*

Son to the Father, being one God, suffereth temptation, and
yieldeth not to the temptation, but suffereth himself to be
mocked, and scourged, and cast out, and disowned by his
people. (Mosiah 15:1–5.)

Properly understood, the text does not combine the personages of the Father and the Son but rather dramatically separates them. As with most men, Christ is both father and son. "Father," modern revelation explains, "because he [the Most High] gave me of his fulness," or as Abinadi described it, "The Father, because he was conceived by the power of God," that is, he inherited from God the capacity to be as God is; "and the Son because I was in the world and made flesh my tabernacle, and dwelt among the sons of men" (D&C 93:4). What Abinadi is teaching us is that the defining characteristic of sonship is flesh while the defining characteristic of the fatherhood is Spirit. Thus he explains that "the will of the Son" is "swallowed up in the will of the Father" so that in all things they act as one. (See Mosiah 15:7.) This captures the essence of the plan of salvation. In like manner, we must each have worked out our salvation to the extent that we have had our own will swallowed up in that of the Father. That is, we are saved to the extent that we are one with him.

For the purpose of this book we are most interested in the announcement that the Son was "conceived by the power of God" and thus was both Son and heir of God's power. Thus the Lord explained to Nephi the son of Nephi, "I come unto my own, to fulfill all things which I have made known unto the children of men from the foundation of the world, and to do the will, both of the Father and of the Son—of the Father because of me, and of the Son because of my flesh" (3 Nephi 1:14).

The Condescension of the Father

In recounting the dream that both he and his father had, Nephi preserves for us what many feel to be the most beautiful account of the birth of Christ we have in holy writ, and certainly the most doctrinally instructive. In this dream both prophets were shown a tree described by Nephi as having a beauty that exceeds all beauty and a whiteness that exceeds "the whiteness of the driven snow" (1 Nephi 11:8). In seeking to understand what the tree represented he was shown a vision, which he described as follows:

> *I looked and beheld the great city of Jerusalem, and also other cities. And I beheld the city of Nazareth; and in the city of Nazareth I beheld a virgin, and she was exceedingly fair and white.*
>
> *And it came to pass that I saw the heavens open; and an angel came down and stood before me; and he said unto me: Nephi, what beholdest thou?*
>
> *And I said unto him: A virgin, most beautiful and fair above all other virgins.*
>
> *And he said unto me: Knowest thou the condescension of God?*
>
> *And I said unto him: I know that he loveth his children; nevertheless, I do not know the meaning of all things.*
>
> *And he said unto me: Behold, the virgin whom thou seest is the mother of the Son of God, after the manner of the flesh.*
>
> *And it came to pass that I beheld that she was carried away in the Spirit; and after she had been carried away in the Spirit for the space of a time the angel spake unto me, saying: Look!*
>
> *And I looked and beheld the virgin again, bearing a child in her arms.*
>
> *And the angel said unto me: Behold the Lamb of God, yea, even the Son of the Eternal Father! Knowest thou the meaning of the tree which thy father saw? (1 Nephi 11:13–21.)*

Thus in response to his inquiry as to the meaning of the tree, Nephi learns that it is a symbolic representation of Christ. Alma uses the same imagery in likening the testimony of the divine sonship of Christ to a seed that if properly nourished grows up into the tree of everlasting life. (See Alma 33:1, 11–23.)

Nephi also learned that the condescension or grace of the Father consisted of his becoming the father of a mortal offspring, born of Mary. All mankind were born first as spirits and can claim God as their father. Christ alone can claim him as the father of his mortal body and is thus known to us as the Only Begotten in the flesh.

President Ezra Taft Benson said: "The Church of Jesus Christ of Latter-day Saints proclaims that Jesus Christ is the Son of God in the most literal sense. The body in which He performed His mission in the flesh was [fathered] by that same Holy Being we worship as God, our Eternal Father. Jesus was not the son of Joseph, nor was He begotten by the Holy Ghost. He is the Son of the Eternal Father!" (*Come unto Christ,* Deseret Book Co., 1983, p. 4.) Similarly, Elder Bruce R. McConkie said: "That is to say, the condescension of God lies in the fact that he, an exalted Being, steps down from his eternal throne to become the Father of a mortal Son, a Son born 'after the manner of the flesh.'" (*The Mortal Messiah,* Deseret Book Co., 1979, 1:314.)

Nephi's testimony is sustained by that of King Benjamin, who in a detailed messianic prophecy given about 124 B.C. stated: "And he shall be called Jesus Christ, the Son of God, the Father of heaven and earth, the Creator of all things from the beginning; and his mother shall be called Mary" (Mosiah 3:8). And again, Alma declared: "And behold, he shall be born of Mary, at Jerusalem which is the land of our forefathers, she being a virgin, a precious and chosen vessel, who shall be overshadowed and conceive by the power of the Holy Ghost, and bring forth a son, yea, even the Son of God" (Alma 7:10).

Let Your Light So Shine

All who have the light of the gospel have been commanded to let that light shine that others might see and, having seen, glorify their Father who is in heaven (see Matthew 5:16; 3 Nephi 12:16; 18:24). We cannot rest the hope of our salvation upon quaint traditions or on philosophical speculations. Ours must be a sure knowledge. Further, there must be a way through which those of us who are separated from the time of the Savior's birth by some two thousand years may still have claim upon the heavens for a sure knowledge of the divine sonship of Christ. For where there is no knowledge of God and his doings there can be no faith in him, and "without faith it is impossible to please him: for he that cometh to God must believe that he is, and that he is a rewarder of them that diligently seek him" (Hebrews 11:6; see also D&C 63:11).

Neither the message nor the messenger can stand alone. "It is for this very reason that the Godhead consists of three separate and distinct personages—two Gods to bear witness of the third. Thus Christ explained: 'I bear record of the Father, and the Father beareth record of me, and the Holy Ghost beareth record of the Father and me' (3 Nephi 11:32)." (Kent P. Jackson and Robert L. Millet, eds., *Studies in Scripture: The Gospels,* Salt Lake City: Deseret Book Co., 1986, 5:284–85.)

No part of the New Testament account of the birth of Christ has escaped the critical eye of Bible scholars. There is nothing in the story that they cannot color with the gray shadows of doubt. All of which makes the splendid light of the Book of Mormon shine more brightly. This is an important part of our story, for it stands at the heart of the principle or doctrine of witnesses. Knowing that the testimony of Bible prophets and writers would be questioned, the Lord preserved, in its purity, a second witness of the divine sonship of Christ and the saving principles of his gospel, to come forth in the last days as a source of light, assurance, and direction for those with believing hearts. Not only does it confirm the ancient law of witnesses but also it teaches that law with plainness and power.

CHAPTER TWO

The Testimony of Angels

*There appeared
unto Zacharias an
angel of the Lord, saying,
"I am Gabriel"*

Angels were the first to announce the birth of Christ. That announcement was made to those of all nations. "Yea, and the voice of the Lord, by the mouth of angels, doth declare it unto all nations; . . . yea, and he doth sound these glad tidings among all his people, yea, even to them that are scattered abroad upon the face of the earth; wherefore they have come unto us," declared Alma (Alma 13:22). All who shared a faith in God were entitled to know that the time of the birth of his Son, the Savior of mankind, had come. In his epistle to the Hebrews the Apostle Paul testified that when the "firstbegotten," or Christ, came into the world, God said, "let all the angels of God worship him" (Hebrews 1:6). Surely the birth of Christ was an occasion upon which the "morning stars" and the "sons of God shouted for joy" (Job 38:7).[1]

The angelic announcements of the birth of Christ as made in the New World were given with sufficient plainness, Alma said, that "we cannot err."

> *And this because of our being wanderers in a strange land; therefore, we are thus highly favored, for we have these glad tidings declared unto us in all parts of our vineyard.*
>
> *For behold, angels are declaring it unto many at this*

time in our land [about 82 B.C.]; and this is for the purpose of preparing the hearts of the children of men to receive his word at the time of his coming in his glory.

And now we only wait to hear the joyful news declared unto us by the mouth of angels, of his coming; for the time cometh, we know not how soon. Would to God that it might be in my day; but let it be sooner or later, in it I will rejoice.

And it shall be made known unto just and holy men, by the mouth of angels, at the time of his coming, that the words of our fathers may be fulfilled, according to that which they have spoken concerning him, which was according to the spirit of prophecy which was in them. (Alma 13:22–26.)

Those to Whom Angels Appear

As part of his concluding testimony in the Book of Mormon, Moroni declared that "God knowing all things, being from everlasting to everlasting, behold, he sent angels to minister unto the children of men, to make manifest concerning the coming of Christ" (Moroni 7:22). Alma, as just noted, told us that angels would bear this message to "just and holy men." For instance, an angel appeared to King Benjamin saying, "I am come to declare unto you the glad tidings of great joy."

For the Lord hath heard thy prayers, and hath judged of thy righteousness, and hath sent me to declare unto thee that thou mayest rejoice; and that thou mayest declare unto thy people, that they may also be filled with joy.

For behold, the time cometh, and is not far distant, that with power, the Lord Omnipotent who reigneth, who was, and is from all eternity to all eternity, shall come down from heaven among the children of men, and shall dwell in a tabernacle of clay, and shall go forth amongst men, working mighty miracles, such as healing the sick, raising the dead, causing the lame to walk, the blind to receive their sight, and the deaf to hear, and curing all manner of diseases.

And he shall cast out devils, or the evil spirits which dwell in the hearts of the children of men.

And lo, he shall suffer temptations, and pain of body, hunger, thirst, and fatigue, even more than man can suffer, except it be unto death; for behold, blood cometh from every pore, so great shall be his anguish for the wickedness and the abominations of his people.

And he shall be called Jesus Christ, the Son of God, the Father of heaven and earth, the Creator of all things from the beginning; and his mother shall be called Mary.

And lo, he cometh unto his own, that salvation might come unto the children of men even through faith on his name; and even after all this they shall consider him a man, and say that he hath a devil, and shall scourge him, and shall crucify him.

And he shall rise the third day from the dead; and behold, he standeth to judge the world; and behold, all these things are done that a righteous judgment might come upon the children of men. (Mosiah 3:3–10.)

Affirming that these things were to be known among all men and women of faith, King Benjamin added: "The Lord God hath sent his holy prophets among all the children of men, to declare these things to every kindred, nation, and tongue, that thereby whosoever should believe that Christ should come, the same might receive remission of their sins, and rejoice with exceedingly great joy, even as though he had already come among them" (Mosiah 3:13).

Let us then consider the scriptural accounts of the appearance of angels heralding the birth of Christ to those of the Old World.

The Righteousness of Zacharias and Elisabeth
(Luke 1:5–7)

There was in the days of Herod, the king of Judaea, a certain priest named Zacharias, of the course of Abia: and

> *his wife was of the daughters of Aaron, and her name was*
> *Elisabeth.*
>
> *And they were both righteous before God, walking in all*
> *the commandments and ordinances of the Lord blameless.*
>
> *And they had no child, because that Elisabeth was bar-*
> *ren, and they both were now well stricken in years.*

As to the "days of Herod," as spoken of by Luke, history records the following: Herod was appointed King of Judea by the Roman Senate in 40 B.C. at the suggestion of Octavian and Antony. He died in 4 B.C. Thus the birth of Christ cannot be placed later than 5 B.C. The date here given by Luke suggests that it must have been 6 or 7 B.C.

Zacharias and Elisabeth, now advanced in years, had not been blessed with children. Having dedicated their lives to the service of God they now searched their souls, wondering if they had offended in some point of the law, for among their people the lack of children was thought to be a divine curse (see Deuteronomy 7:14).

Gabriel Appears to Zacharias
(Luke 1:8–11)

> *And it came to pass, that while he executed the priest's*
> *office before God in the order of his course [priesthood, JST],*
>
> *According to the custom [law, JST] of the priest's office,*
> *his lot was to burn incense when he went into the temple of*
> *the Lord.*
>
> *And the whole multitude of the people were praying*
> *without at the time of incense.*
>
> *And there appeared unto him an angel of the Lord*
> *standing on the right side of the altar of incense.*

The descendants of Aaron were divided into twenty-four courses or family divisions. Zacharias was of the family of Abijah (or Abia as rendered in Greek). In Hebrew the name means "my father is Jehovah." Twice a year, in the months of April and October, Zacharias would join those of his family or course in the temple, where they would labor in their priestly duties for eight days, a period embracing two Sabbaths. They would then return to their village, assuming again their occupations. Upon arrival at the temple they would draw lots to determine what duties would be theirs. The greatest honor that could befall a priest was to draw that lot assigning him to attend the altar of incense in the holy place. The duties or lots numbered near a thousand, and a man having drawn the privilege of attending the sacred altar was never again to be eligible for this singular honor. It was not by chance that Zacharias drew this lot. This duty was performed twice daily, at the morning and the evening sacrifice. When Zacharias entered the holy place "the whole multitude of the people were praying without at the time of incense."

The united prayer of the nation, the ascension of which was represented symbolically by the flame and smoke from the altar of incense, was for the coming of their Messiah, who would, as they believed, liberate them from their Roman bondage. Zacharias would also have prayed for the coming of the promised Messiah, but to his prayer he appended an appeal for a son, one to whom he could pass the priesthood he held and through whom he could keep alive the promises made to those of his family.

While Zacharias attended to the altar of incense, Gabriel appeared to him. Properly, the angel stood on the right of the altar, which is known as the place of honor.

The Birth of John Announced
(Luke 1:12–14)

And when Zacharias saw him, he was troubled, and fear fell upon him.

But the angel said unto him, Fear not, Zacharias: for thy prayer is heard; and thy wife Elisabeth shall bear thee a son, and thou shalt call his name John.

*And thou shalt have joy and gladness; and many shall
rejoice at his birth.*

The fear felt by Zacharias would have been that of reverential
awe. His life had been such that he had no reason to suppose he
was unworthy of such a manifestation.

Confirmation was now given that the prayer of a lifetime was
to be realized. The curse of barrenness was to be lifted from the
devout couple and the authority of heaven with its attendant
blessings was to continue in their lineage. In this miraculous
birth Elisabeth and Zacharias became types of the blessing that
would be accorded to all who were just and holy among their nation. They too would have the curse of spiritual barrenness lifted
from them by a Son of miraculous birth, and they too would
then enjoy the fulness of heaven's blessings.

For both the dispensation of Christ's ministry and the dispensation of the fulness of times John alone held the authority
by which the way is prepared for the coming of Christ. None can
receive the Messiah save they first receive a remission of sins
under the direction of the keys held by the Baptist. One cannot
rejoice in the promise of salvation without rejoicing in the ministry of John.

John to Be Filled with the Holy Ghost
(Luke 1:15)

*For he shall be great in the sight of the Lord, and shall
drink neither wine nor strong drink; and he shall be filled
with the Holy Ghost, even from his mother's womb.*

Of the son born to Zacharias the Lord himself would yet say,
"Among those that are born of women there is not a greater
prophet than John the Baptist" (Luke 7:28). According to Numbers 6:3, Nazarites were forbidden the use of wine or strong
drink—the latter being an inclusive term for an intoxicating
drink.

As far as our present scriptures record, none but John have been accorded the privilege of the companionship of the Holy Ghost while yet in their mother's womb (see D&C 84:27). Elder Bruce R. McConkie wrote: "Implicit in this divine assurance is the prophecy that John would be true to his mission as a witness of Christ and would endure all his days in faith and righteousness. Otherwise he would not remain filled with the Spirit. Because of this special endowment, John, yet unborn and while literally in his mother's womb, recognized and saluted the mother of Jesus. (Luke 1:39–45.)" (*Doctrinal New Testament Commentary,* Salt Lake City: Bookcraft, 1965, 1:79.)

John to Prepare the Way for Christ
(Luke 1:16–17)

And many of the children of Israel shall he turn to the Lord their God.

And he shall go before him in the spirit and power of Elias, to turn the hearts of the fathers to the children, and the disobedient to the wisdom of the just; to make ready a people prepared for the Lord.

The idea of "turning," or "returning" is standard Old Testament language for repentance. John's doctrine was that of repentance and baptism. Among those that he turned to the Lord were the original Twelve, who, with the possible exception of Judas, followed him before they followed Christ. When filling the vacancy in their number after Judas's betrayal the Apostles made their choice from among those who had also first been followers of John. (See Acts 1:21–22.)

This is the Elias of whom the Savior said, "I send [him] to prepare the way before me" (JST Matthew 17:13–14). An Elias is a forerunner. Such is the office and power of the Aaronic Priesthood—to prepare the way for that which is greater. The gospel brings a welding link between the generations. Thus the hopes of righteous fathers in generations past find realization in their posterity as they return to the faith.

Zacharias Doubts the Words of Gabriel
(Luke 1:18–20)

*And Zacharias said unto the angel, Whereby shall I
know this? for I am an old man, and my wife well stricken
in years.*

*And the angel answering said unto him, I am Gabriel,
that stand in the presence of God; and am sent to speak
unto thee, and to shew thee these glad tidings.*

*And, behold, thou shalt be dumb, and not able to speak,
until the day that these things shall be performed, because
thou believest not my words, which shall be fulfilled in their
season.*

Zacharias' demand for a sign "whereby" he might know with
certainty of Gabriel's message hardly kept with the spirit of his
prayer. As the spirit of doubt had cut his people off from the
blessings of heaven for so many years it would now cut him off
from communication with the believer and unbeliever alike for a
period of more than nine months.

In response to Zacharias' doubt the angel introduced himself
so as to identify the authority by which he spoke. "I am
Gabriel," he said, literally meaning "Man of God," and I "stand
in the presence of God"! That is "I speak the words of God." We
can but suppose that the tone of this response was such as to
make Zacharias' very bones quake.

A sign was then given—Zacharias was to be left without
speech until after the child of promise had been born.

Zacharias Returns to Elisabeth
(Luke 1:21–23)

*And the people waited for Zacharias, and marveled
that he tarried so long in the temple.*

*And when he came out, he could not speak unto them:
and they perceived that he had seen a vision in the temple:
for he beckoned unto them, and remained speechless.*

And it came to pass, that, as soon as the days of his min-
istration were accomplished, he departed to his own house.

The people outside the holy place were waiting for the priest
to come out in order to chant the hymn that accompanied the
sacrifice to be offered on the altar of holocausts, and they wondered at this extraordinary delay. Finally, Zacharias appeared on
the threshold, but he did not pronounce the customary benediction over the people, nor could he speak to them; thus they could
but suppose that he had experienced a divine manifestation.

The Story Evidences Its Own Truthfulness

The most careful deliberation by the best of scholars could
not have produced a more fitting or perfect story to introduce
the birth and ministry of Christ than that recorded by Luke.
Centuries earlier Malachi had prophesied that a messenger would
be sent to prepare the way for the Messiah who himself would be
the messenger of the covenant or harbinger of salvation (see
Malachi 3:1; D&C 93:8). Anciently it was the practice for a messenger to go before the king to announce his coming and to
make all necessary arrangements for him. It has ever been the
duty of the Aaronic, or preparatory, Priesthood to act as an Elias
to announce the coming of Christ and to see that there is a people prepared to receive him. Despite the corruption of that
priesthood in the meridian day, as witnessed in the behavior of
those who held the office of high priest, it rested in its purity in
Zacharias—a just and holy man worthy to entertain angels. Thus
it was that Gabriel, second in the hierarchy of angels only to
Adam himself, appeared to this humble priest to announce that
his prayer had been heard and that the issue of his loins, bearing
the priesthood that he held, would herald the long-sought coming of the Messiah. Let us consider how naturally and perfectly
the story unfolds.

Where, we might ask, should the announcement of the birth
of Christ be made? To which we would answer, Jerusalem or the

City of the Lord, the very city from which we have been told that the word of the Lord should go forth (see Isaiah 2:3). And where in that City so laden with history should the announcement come forth? Why, at the temple, of course, on holy ground—ground upon which men come seeking their God. And where in the temple, we would then ask, should such an announcement be made? The holy place next to altar of incense, would be our answer, for the smoke that ascends therefrom symbolizes the ascending prayers of a nation praying for the coming of their Messiah. And at what hour should this event take place? At the time of public prayer when the host of Israel unite in importuning the heavens that they might realize the promise of the coming of their Messiah. And who, we might ask, should bear that message? An angel of the Lord, one who had stood in the divine presence!

Should this unembodied spirit come from the realms of those yet to be born in our pre-earth estate or from among the faithful who had once sojourned upon this earth? Why, from among the faithful who bore the curse of Adam's fall. Ought it not be one of Israel's faithful fathers? Assuredly it should. If not father Adam himself, then Noah, who was also father of all. And thus it was that Gabriel—once known to us as Noah—appeared to declare these grand tidings. To whom should he come? Was it to one of the corrupt temple priests who laid claim to his office through political wrangling and who sought the pleasure of Rome, or to a lay priest whose lineage reached back in purity to Aaron, from whence he traced his priesthood and the right to stand at its head?[2] The question answers itself. It must be a humble priest of Aaron. And thus it was that Gabriel appeared with his heaven-sent message to Zacharias in the manner described by Luke.

Gabriel Appears to Mary

We will consider the scriptural account of Gabriel's visit with Mary in chapter four, "Handmaidens of the Lord." At this point let it suffice to say that angels come to men, women, and children to impart the word of God (see Alma 32:23). Of Gabriel's visit to Mary, Elder McConkie said, "Never was there a case when angelic ministration was more deserved, or served a greater purpose, or was manifest in a sweeter and more tender way, than when Gabriel, who stands in the presence of God, came to Mary to announce her divine call to be the mother of the Son of God." (*The Mortal Messiah* 1:317.) In that visit, known as the Annunciation, Mary learned that she had been chosen to be the mother of the Son of God.

An Angel Appears to Joseph
(Matthew 1:18)

Now the birth of Jesus Christ was on this wise: When as his mother Mary was espoused to Joseph, before they came together, she was found with child of the Holy Ghost.

Mary, while espoused to Joseph but before they were formally married, "was found with child." This suggests that she did not volunteer information relative to her state but rather let it be discovered. Nor should it be supposed that Mary told Joseph that she carried the "child of the Holy Ghost." The nature of the conception of the child was made known to Joseph by the angel in a dream. He did not learn it from Mary. Matthew, however, in recording the story does not want the reader, even for a moment, to think of the child as anything other than divinely conceived, though some characters in the story would not know this at this time.

The statement of Matthew, as recorded here, that Mary was with child "of the Holy Ghost" has caused endless confusion. Christ is not the child of the Holy Ghost. He is the Son of God! It would properly be said that Mary was with child "by the power of the Holy Ghost." Both Luke and Alma record the matter this way. The language of Gabriel, according to Luke, was: "The Holy Ghost shall come upon thee, and the power of the Highest shall overshadow thee" (Luke 1:35). Alma chose this language to teach the principle: "The Son of God cometh upon the face of the earth," Alma testified, "And behold, he shall be born of Mary, . . . she being a virgin, a precious and chosen vessel, who shall be overshadowed and conceive by the power of the Holy Ghost, and bring forth a son, yea, even the Son of God." (Alma 7:9–10.)

Joseph's Prayer Is Answered
(Matthew 1:19–20)

Then Joseph her husband, being a just man, and not willing to make her a publick example, was minded to put her away privily.

But while he thought on these things, behold, the angel of the Lord appeared unto him in a dream, saying, Joseph, thou son of David, fear not to take unto thee Mary thy wife: for that which is conceived in her is of the Holy Ghost.

It was both the right and the duty of an observant Jew who believed his wife to be guilty of an extra-marital sexual sin to give her a bill of divorcement (see Deuteronomy 24:1). Joseph as a "just man," that is, one observant of the law, would be expected to do so. It was precisely for this reason that he "was minded to put her away privily," meaning, to legally divorce Mary but in a private or secret manner. This Joseph did, not because he disdained the law, but rather in order to fulfil the law without subjecting Mary to public humiliation. It is here that we discover the measure of Joseph's love for his espoused wife.

Joseph, driven to his knees in despair, undoubtedly sought divine help. If Zacharias could pray for a son, Joseph could pray for understanding as to what to do about his espoused wife. The thought that there was no such thing as personal revelation had not occurred to those of that day. The divine plan called for Joseph to know of Mary's conception and to know from the same source by which she knew. Nothing other than revelation would suffice, for he too was to be a special witness of the birth of God's Son. It was only with the blessing of heaven that Joseph took Mary as wife and the Holy Family became complete. Joseph's role was absolutely essential in protecting and providing for Mary and her son. Further, it was his destiny to be a role model and mentor to Jesus during his ever-important youthful years.

The angel of the Lord appeared to Joseph in a dream saying, "Joseph, thou son of David"—for Joseph, like Mary, was of the house and lineage of Israel's greatest king—"Fear not to take unto thee Mary thy wife: for that which is conceived in her is [by the power] of the Holy Ghost. And she shall bring forth a son, and thou shalt call his name Jesus: for he shall save his people from their sins." (Matthew 2:20–21.)

"Joseph now knew! Doubt fled. The circle of true believers was growing. He had the same testimony, from the same source, as did Mary and Elisabeth and Zacharias; and, according to their law, in the mouths of two or three witnesses shall every word be established. The Lord was providing his witnesses, and soon the whole nation and the whole world would be bound to believe, and that at the peril of their salvation. How often Joseph bore the special witness that was his we do not know, but that he remained true to every trust and that he performed the mission assigned him by the Lord, there can be no doubt." (Bruce R. McConkie, *The Mortal Messiah,* 1:332–33.)

The Messiah to Be Named Jesus
(Matthew 1:21)

And she shall bring forth a son, and thou shalt call his name JESUS: for he shall save his people from their sins.

The name *Jesus,* which the child was to receive, had already been communicated to his mother (see Luke 1:31). Matthew explains the meaning of the name to be "he shall save his people from their sins." A more literal etymology might be "Jehovah saves." The name Jesus Christ combines the personal name Jesus with the title Christ, meaning "the Anointed One."

The Words of Isaiah Fulfilled
(Matthew 1:22–23)

*Now all this was done, that it might be fulfilled which
was spoken of the Lord by the prophet, saying,
Behold, a virgin shall be with child, and shall bring
forth a son, and they shall call his name Emmanuel, which
being interpreted is, God with us.*

Matthew draws upon the words of Isaiah to dramatize the
miraculous nature of Christ's birth. Mary was a virgin until after
the birth of Christ, for no mortal man was father to her child.
Thereafter she and Joseph enjoyed the privilege of parenthood.

Joseph Takes Mary as His Wife
(Matthew 1:24–25)

*Then Joseph being raised from sleep did as the angel of
the Lord had bidden him, and took unto him his wife:
And knew her not till she had brought forth her firstborn son: and he called his name JESUS.*

Mary, in her delicate and socially embarrassing situation,
sought refuge with Elisabeth in the hill country of Judea. It was
during this three-month period that Joseph wrestled with the
Spirit in search of direction. Following this dream he immediately sent for Mary, asking her to take her rightful place at his
side. The phrase "took unto him his wife," is rendered by some
translators as "took his wife home" (see Moffatt's & Brown's
translations), this being the custom of the day. We can but imagine the relief and joy felt by Mary when Joseph sent for her. Thus
the Christ child was born in wedlock.

Notwithstanding their married state, the couple refrained
from sexual union until after the birth of Christ. Thereafter Mary
became the mother of both sons and daughters. Though the
names of his sisters have not been preserved for us we know that

the Savior's half-brothers were James, Joseph, Simon, and Judas (see Matthew 13:55–56).

The Testimony of Angels

From the days of Adam the gospel has been declared by angels (see Moses 5:58). Teaching father Adam the purpose of the law of sacrifice, the angel of the Lord explained: "This thing is a similitude of the sacrifice of the Only Begotten of the Father, which is full of grace and truth. Wherefore, thou shalt do all that thou doest in the name of the Son, and thou shalt repent and call upon God in the name of the Son forevermore." (Moses 5:7–8.) The Apostle Paul declared that angels minister to them who "shall be heirs of salvation" (JST Hebrews 1:14). In our dispensation all who receive any blessing at the hands of the priesthood are receiving it through authority restored by angels. As we have that authority at their hands, so we have their testimony relative to the most central doctrines of the plan of salvation—both the birth and the resurrection of God's Son.

NOTES

1. It appears that Paul is quoting from memory and mixing two texts found in the Septuagint (see *The Interpreter's Bible*, 11:605). Non-LDS commentaries struggle with all texts that refer to our premortal existence. Without a knowledge of the pre-earth life neither the reference to Christ as the "first-born" nor the passage in Job make any sense.

2. The idea for this paragraph came from *Clarke's Commentary* 1:357.

CHAPTER THREE

The Testimony of the Baptist

Zacharias prophesied, "Thou, child, shalt be called the prophet of the Highest"

Jesus of Nazareth spoke of no man with greater respect than he did of John the Baptist. To those who had gone down to Jordan to hear John preach, the Savior asked: "What went ye out into the wilderness to see? A reed shaken with the wind? But what went ye out for to see? A man clothed in soft raiment? behold, they that wear soft clothing are in kings' houses. But what went ye out for to see? A prophet? Yea, I say unto you, and more than a prophet. For this is he, of whom it is written, Behold, I send my messenger before thy face, which shall prepare thy way before thee. Verily I say unto you, Among them that are born of women there hath not risen a greater than John the Baptist." (Matthew 11:7–11.)

We have more prophetic references to the ministry of John the Baptist by the writers of scripture than we do for any prophet save Jesus only. Isaiah and Malachi both foreshadowed his ministry in the Old World. Lehi and Nephi did the same for those in the New World. And the angel Gabriel described John's meridian ministry to his father, Zacharias, who in turn gave a prophetic blessing to his son. Significantly, each of these prophecies also embraced events that were central to the restoration of the priesthood in our day. In addition to this, during his ministry among the Nephites the resurrected Christ foreshadowed the role of the Baptist in the latter-day restoration (see 3 Nephi 24:1, 3). All of this becomes important to the story we now tell of John's special role as a witness of Christ's divine sonship and as the one ordained in the councils of heaven to prepare the way for the Lord.

John As Spoken of by Isaiah and Malachi

Isaiah wrote of "The voice of him that crieth in the wilderness, Prepare ye the way of the Lord, make straight in the desert a highway for our God." Such was the office and calling of John the Baptist (see Matthew 3:3; Mark 1:3; Luke 3:4). Long before he was born on earth John was commissioned in the councils of heaven to prepare the way for the Savior. "Every valley shall be exalted, and every mountain and hill shall be made low: and the crooked shall be made straight, and the rough places plain: and the glory of the Lord shall be revealed, and all flesh shall see it together: for the mouth of the Lord hath spoken it." (Isaiah 40:3–5.) A more complete and instructive rendering of Isaiah's words was restored to us by Joseph Smith in the Joseph Smith Translation. It reads as follows:

> *As it is written in the book of the prophet Esaias; and these are the words, saying, The voice of one crying in the wilderness, Prepare ye the way of the Lord, and make his paths straight.*
>
> *For behold, and lo, he shall come, as it is written in the book of the prophets, to take away the sins of the world, and to bring salvation unto the heathen nations, to gather together those who are lost, who are of the sheepfold of Israel;*
>
> *Yea, even the dispersed and afflicted; and also to prepare the way, and make possible the preaching of the gospel unto the Gentiles;*
>
> *And to be a light unto all who sit in darkness, unto the uttermost parts of the earth; to bring to pass the resurrection from the dead, and to ascend up on high, to dwell on the right hand of the Father,*

Until the fulness of time, and the law and the testimony shall be sealed, and the keys of the kingdom shall be delivered up again unto the Father;

To administer justice unto all; to come down in judgment upon all, and to convince all the ungodly of their ungodly deeds, which they have committed; and all this in the day that he shall come;

For it is a day of power; yea, every valley shall be filled, and every mountain and hill shall be brought low; the crooked shall be made straight, and the rough ways made smooth. (JST Luke 3:4–10.)

This restoration of text expands our view of the understanding and testimony of the Baptist as he heralded the ministry of Christ. As a voice in the wilderness he called for all to prepare for the Messiah's coming, that in all things we might be ready to receive him. The Messiah, John testified, was to bear the sins of the world, bring salvation to the Gentile nations, and gather scattered Israel. Nor would his ministry end there, for he would also take the glad tidings of the gospel to those in the darkness of the "uttermost parts of the earth," presumably meaning the world of the spirits. All were to hear the message, both the living and the dead.

John knew well that all this would not be accomplished in the mortal ministry of the Lord, for there would be a season in which the testimony would be "sealed" to come forth again in a final great gospel dispensation, in which the Messiah would come again in power and glory, and in which all things would conform to his will, including the elements of the earth. John would also have understood that it would be his office and calling in this the last dispensation to once again prepare the way for the Lord.

Malachi gives another prophetic description of the office and call of the Baptist.

Behold, I will send my messenger, and he shall prepare the way before me: and the Lord, whom ye seek, shall suddenly

*come to his temple, even the messenger of the covenant,
whom ye delight in: behold, he shall come, saith the Lord of
hosts.*

*But who may abide the day of his coming? and who
shall stand when he appeareth? for he is like a refiner's fire,
and like a fullers' soap:*

*And he shall sit as a refiner and purifier of silver: and
he shall purify the sons of Levi, and purge them as gold and
silver, that they may offer unto the Lord an offering in
righteousness.*

*Then shall the offering of Judah and Jerusalem be
pleasant unto the Lord, as in the days of old, and as in for-
mer years. (Malachi 3:1–4.)*

The context of this passage, though ignored by non-LDS
commentaries, is the Second Coming. At this time a messenger,
John the Baptist, is to come to prepare the way for the Lord to
make his "sudden" visit to his temple. In this day, only those
who have been cleansed or purged from sin—following the manner of purification known to the ancients—will be able to endure
his presence. This explains why the temple will be the place of his
coming. It would have had to be obvious to John, who knew
and quoted this and the Isaiah prophecy, that though an applica-
tion of these prophecies could be made to his mortal ministry,
he, like Christ, must come again to the earth to complete all that
was being described in the prophetic word (see Matthew 11:10;
Mark 1:2).

That others of John's day also understood that the Baptist
would be numbered among the ancient prophets who would return as part of a great restoration of all things is evidenced by the
report given to Christ by his disciples when he inquired of them
who men said he was. This occurred more than two years after
the death of the Baptist. Matthew records the incident thus:
"When Jesus came into the coasts of Caesarea Philippi, he asked
his disciples, saying, Whom do men say that I the Son of Man
am? And they said, Some say that thou art John the Baptist:

some, Elias; and others, Jeremias, or one of the prophets."
(Matthew 16:13–14.) Well-established traditions also existed announcing the return of Elias (Elijah) and Jeremiah (see Malachi
4:5–6; 2 Maccabees 2:1–8).

John As Known Among the Nephites

In Father Lehi's magnificent vision of the destiny of the
house of Israel he saw the mission and ministry of John the Baptist, of which he gave a partial description, including even some
of the very words John would speak. In 1 Nephi 8:7–10 we read
as follows:

> *And he spake also concerning a prophet who should
> come before the Messiah, to prepare the way of the Lord—*
> *Yea, even he should go forth and cry in the wilderness:
> Prepare ye the way of the Lord, and make his paths straight;
> for there standeth one among you whom ye know not; and
> he is mightier than I, whose shoe's latchet I am not worthy
> to unloose. And much spake my father concerning this
> thing.*
> *And my father said he should baptize in Bethabara, be-
> yond Jordan; and he also said he should baptize with water;
> even that he should baptize the Messiah with water.*
> *And after he had baptized the Messiah with water, he
> should behold and bear record that he had baptized the
> Lamb of God, who should take away the sins of the world.*

Nephi, who was shown the same vision as his father, gives an
extended commentary on the baptism of Christ and the necessity
for it. We read this in 2 Nephi.

> *And now, if the Lamb of God, he being holy, should
> have need to be baptized by water, to fulfil all righteousness,
> O then, how much more need have we, being unholy, to be
> baptized, yea, even by water!*

> *And now, I would ask of you, my beloved brethren,*
> *wherein the Lamb of God did fulfil all righteousness in*
> *being baptized by water?*
>
> *Know ye not that he was holy? But notwithstanding he*
> *being holy, he showeth unto the children of men that, ac-*
> *cording to the flesh he humbleth himself before the Father,*
> *and witnesseth unto the Father that he would be obedient*
> *unto him in keeping his commandments.*
>
> *Wherefore, after he was baptized with water the Holy*
> *Ghost descended upon him in the form of a dove.*
>
> *And again, it showeth unto the children of men the*
> *straitness of the path, and the narrowness of the gate, by*
> *which they should enter, he having set the example before*
> *them.*
>
> *And he said unto the children of men: Follow thou me.*
> *Wherefore, my beloved brethren, can we follow Jesus save we*
> *shall be willing to keep the commandments of the Father?*
>
> *And the Father said: Repent ye, repent ye, and be bap-*
> *tized in the name of my Beloved Son. (2 Nephi 31:5–11.)*

Nephi's entire discourse could profitably be cited here. We will, however, let this extract suffice for our purpose. From this we learn that it was necessary for the Savior to be baptized, and, for that matter, to conform to all the ordinances of the gospel, in order to work out his own salvation and in order that he might say to all others, "Follow me." All who desire a place in the kingdom of heaven, Nephi taught, must be baptized according to the command of the Father "in the name" of his "Beloved Son." Thus the ordinance of baptism itself becomes a witness of the doctrine of divine sonship.

What Manner of Child Shall This Be!
(Luke 1:59–66)

> *And it came to pass, that on the eighth day they came to*
> *circumcise the child; and they called him Zacharias, after*
> *the name of his father.*

And his mother answered and said, Not so; but he shall be called John.

And they said unto her, There is none of thy kindred that is called by this name.

And they made signs to his father, how he would have him called.

And he asked for a writing table, and wrote, saying, His name is John. And they marveled all.

And his mouth was opened immediately, and his tongue loosed, and he spake, and praised God.

And fear came on all that dwelt round about them: and all these sayings were noised abroad throughout all the hill country of Judaea.

And all they that heard them laid them up in their hearts, saying, What manner of child shall this be! And the hand of the Lord was with him.

On the eighth day after the birth of this child of destiny family and friends gathered to witness his circumcision, by which he would be consecrated to God and become an heir of the covenant. Those assembled were already calling him Zacharias, supposing that this would be the name given him to show honor to his stricken father. In some instances a son was given his father's name, but the greater precedence favored giving the name of a grandfather. Elisabeth's announcement that his name was to be John came as a surprise. Others made signs to the mute Zacharias, who may also have been deaf. He responded by taking a "writing table," meaning a piece of wood with wax on it, and writing the name *John*, in accordance with Gabriel's instruction.

It was intended that inspiration attend the giving of a name. It was more than a matter of coincidence that many of the key characters in the Bible bore names that prophetically described or memorialized their ministry. The name John, which means, "God has shown favor," or "Jehovah is gracious," is appropriate both for the circumstances of the Baptist's birth and the purpose of his ministry to prepare the way for the Messiah. It was at this point in the drama that speech was restored to Zacharias, who then with great power blessed his son and praised God. This, coupled with the unusual nature of his birth, left those present to wonder, "What manner of child shall this be!"

The Promise of a Redeemer Given to the Fathers
(Luke 1:67–75)

> *And his father Zacharias was filled with the Holy Ghost, and prophesied, saying,*
>
> *Blessed be the Lord God of Israel; for he hath visited and redeemed his people,*
>
> *And hath raised up an horn of salvation for us in the house of his servant David;*
>
> *As he spake by the mouth of his holy prophets, which have been since the world began:*
>
> *That we should be saved from our enemies, and from the hand of all that hate us;*
>
> *To perform the mercy promised to our fathers, and to remember his holy covenant;*
>
> *The oath which he sware to our father Abraham,*
>
> *That he would grant unto us, that we being delivered out of the hand of our enemies might serve him without fear,*
>
> *In holiness and righteousness before him, all the days of our life.*

In this inspired psalm known as the Benedictus, Zacharias ties the hopes and promises given to the fathers to the events that are about to transpire. With the confidence that is associated with the spirit of prophecy he speaks of that which is about to happen—the coming of God to earth and the redemption of Israel—as if it had already happened.

Zacharias depicts Christ as the "horn of salvation." The horn is a symbol of power and strength. It is an offensive weapon and thus depicts the "strength of salvation" or "power of salvation" that is to be found in Christ. He also reaffirms that the promised

Messiah is to come through the lineage of David and to be the rightful heir of his throne.

This coming of the Redeemer to the earth represents the testimony of all the holy prophets since the world began. All prophets who lived before Zacharias have looked to these events.

The understanding that the nation of Israel lays claim to the covenants and promises made by God to their fathers only in "holiness and righteousness" has long been lost to those of our generation. Zacharias prophetically describes our redemption from all our enemies, the greatest of which is our bondage to sin—which is anything that would make us unclean and thus unworthy to stand in the presence of our God.

John to Restore the True Baptism
(Luke 1:76–79)

And thou, child, shalt be called the prophet of the Highest: for thou shalt go before the face of the Lord to prepare his ways;

To give knowledge of salvation unto his people by [baptism for—JST] the remission of their sins,

Through the tender mercy of our God; whereby the dayspring from on high hath visited us,

To give light to them that sit in darkness and in the shadow of death, to guide our feet into the way of peace.

What Zacharias is doing here is very much the same thing as what is known to Latter-day Saints as a father's blessing. In an earlier generation this blessing was often given on the eighth day of the child's life. In it the father gives the child both a name and an inspired blessing. Having announced the child's name to be John, Zacharias now prophesies not only that he will "be called the prophet of the Highest," but also that his charge will be to prepare the way before the Lord, and that he will give the knowledge of salvation unto His people. Here the Joseph Smith Translation adds the word *baptism*. Thus one comes to the knowledge of salvation only as he enters into the covenant that Christ comes to restore. This same covenant was known to their fathers—the covenant of baptism, wherein they took his name upon them. Today missionaries are being sent to all the nations of the earth to gather Israel, which gathering brings them to the waters of baptism, this being the covenant of salvation in all dispensations (see D&C 49:9; 137:6).

The reference to Christ as the "dayspring from on high" is simply a poetic way of announcing the dawning of a new light or the coming of a new day of hope for Israel. It can be argued that Zacharias was referring to John as the "dayspring" in that he was as the morning light preparing us for the glory of the noonday sun. Objection need not be taken to such a title as long as Christ is seen as the source of all light.

The Youthful Years of John
(Luke 1:80)

And the child grew, and waxed strong in spirit, and was in the deserts till the day of his shewing unto Israel.

A statement attributed to Joseph Smith holds that Zacharias, learning of Herod's edict to destroy any child who might be the promised Messiah, had his son, John, taken into the mountains, where he was raised on locusts and wild honey. When Zacharias refused to disclose the child's hiding place, he was killed by Herod's order. His murder is said to have taken place in the Temple between the porch and the altar. (See *Teachings,* 261.) The statement is commentary on Matthew 23:35, in which Christ, at the conclusion of his ministry, speaking of those who have rejected him, says, "That upon you may come all the righteous blood shed upon the earth, from the blood of righteous Abel unto the blood of Zacharias son of Barachias, whom ye slew between the temple and the altar."

The statement originally appeared in an issue of *The Times and Seasons.* Joseph Smith was absent at the time, which suggests to some scholars the possibility that John Taylor, who was then the editor, wrote it in the Prophet's behalf. There are two major difficulties about the statement, one doctrinal, the other historical. The doctrinal concern centers in the justice of Christ in holding the Jews responsible for the slaying of Zacharias when Herod was his murderer. A possible response to this could be that "the chief priests and scribes" who willingly told Herod that the Messiah was to be born in Bethlehem did so to preserve their own power among the Jews—even if it meant killing the Messiah they professed to represent. The historical difficulty centers in the idea that Zacharias could somehow have been appointed by these same people to be the chief priest and thus be found laboring in the temple by Herod's soldiers as the statement suggests. There is no question that the office was rightfully his. The question is would such men have surrendered it to him?

John Ordained by an Angel

In a revelation on the priesthood given to the Prophet Joseph Smith we are told this about the Baptist: "He was baptized while he was yet in his childhood, and was ordained by the angel of God at the time he was eight days old unto this power, to overthrow the kingdom of the Jews, and to make straight the way of the Lord before the face of his people, to prepare them for the coming of the Lord, in whose hand is given all power" (D&C 84:28).

The announcement that John was baptized "in his childhood" does not mean infancy. John would have been baptized when he was eight years of age. Infant baptism is "solemn mockery before God," which denies the atonement of Christ (see Moroni 8:9, 20). To say that John was "ordained" when eight days of age is not to suggest that he received the priesthood at that time. The word *ordained* is frequently used in the Doctrine and Covenants to identify something being designated for a certain purpose without suggesting a conferral of authority. For instance, the Prophet's wife, Emma, was "ordained" to teach and exhort (D&C 25:7), gospel ordinances were "ordained" (D&C 49:15), doctrines were "ordained" (D&C 76:13), beasts and fowls were "ordained" for man's use (D&C 49:19), sons of perdition were "ordained" unto their condemnation (D&C 76:48), and wholesome herbs and grain were "ordained" for the use of man (D&C 89:10, 14).

We do not know at what age John received the priesthood or who conferred it upon him. We know that it was after he was eight years of age and after he had been baptized, and that he could trace his priesthood back to Aaron. We also know that he had the authority to declare the preparatory gospel—faith, repentance, and baptism—and that he held the keys of the ministering of angels (see D&C 84:26–27). What we learn from the Doctrine and Covenants is that the angel of the Lord gave him the charge to "overthrow the kingdom of the Jews," meaning the system of priesthood and government that then held sway among them.

The Office and Call of the Baptist

The ordinance of baptism was not new to the nation of Israel when John appeared on the scene. Through the revelations of the Restoration we can trace the ordinance back to the days of Adam (see Moses 6:52, 64–65). We baptize today by authority restored to us by John the Baptist, who in turn traced his right to perform that ordinance through the generations to Aaron. John was baptized in his youth as were virtually all others in the household of faith (see D&C 84:26–28). "It goes without saying," observed Elder Bruce R. McConkie, "that Zacharias and his fellow priests were baptized. We cannot do other than believe that Elisabeth, Mary, Joseph, Simeon, Anna, the shepherds who heard the heavenly choirs, and hosts of others who waited patiently for the Consolation of Israel had also partaken of this sacred ordinance, all before the ministry of John ever began." (*The Mortal Messiah*, 1:396–97.) The authority by which those baptisms were performed was honored in heaven.

How, then, did the baptism of John differ from that baptism already known to Jews of his day? The difference was simply a matter of authority. John was the rightful heir to Aaron's seat. He held the keys, or right of presidency, over this and all other ordinances performed by the Aaronic, or lesser, Priesthood. His office, which was lineal, traced from father to son to the very origins of the Aaronic Priesthood. It was for this reason, Joseph Smith told us, that "Zacharias pleaded with the Lord in the temple that he might have seed, so that the priesthood might be preserved."[1] Had Zacharias and Elisabeth not given birth to a son, this sacred office would have been lost.

Explaining this principle Joseph Smith said: "The priesthood was given to Aaron and his posterity throughout all generations. We can trace the lineage down to Zacharias, he being the only lawful administrator in his day. And the Jews knew it well, for they always acknowledged the priesthood. Zacharias, having no children, knew that the promise of God must fail. Consequently, he went into the temple to wrestle with God, according to the order of the priesthood, to obtain a promise of a son." (Kent P. Jackson, ed., *Joseph Smith's Commentary on the Bible*, Salt Lake City: Deseret Book, 1994, p. 119.)

John's office was "to overthrow the kingdom of the Jews, and to make straight the way of the Lord before the face of his people, to prepare them for the coming of the Lord, in whose hand is given all power" (D&C 84:28). The baptism of John represented the beginning of a new gospel dispensation. All who had previously been baptized were, with the coming of Christ, to demonstrate their willingness to let go of the preparatory law and embrace the fulness through rebaptism.

What was to take place in the Old World found a perfect reflection in the New World, where the newly called Twelve Apostles were commissioned to rebaptize the nation of the Nephites as they let go of the old order of things to embrace the fulness of Christ (see 3 Nephi 11:21–41). As John stood in the position once known to Aaron, so Christ stood in the position to which Moses had been the type and shadow—the great high priest of

Israel. Again Joseph Smith explains: "John was a priest after the order of Aaron and had the keys of that priesthood. [He] came forth preaching repentance and baptism for the remission of sins but at the same time cried out, 'There cometh one after me mightier than I, the latchet of whose shoes I am not worthy to unloose.' Christ came according to the word of John. He was greater than John, because he held the keys of the Melchizedek Priesthood and the kingdom of God and had before revealed the priesthood to Moses. Yet Christ was baptized by John to fulfill all righteousness." (Jackson, *Joseph Smith's Commentary on the Bible,* pp. 119–120.)

Christ came to fulfill the law, not to destroy it. Joseph Smith explained that "Christ fulfilled all righteousness in becoming obedient to the law which [he] himself had given to Moses on the mount and thereby magnified it and made it honorable instead of destroying it" (Andrew F. Ehat and Lyndon W. Cook, eds., *The Words of Joseph Smith,* Religious Studies Center, BYU, 1980, pp. 162–63.)

> *The question arose from the saying of Jesus—"Among those that are born of women there is not a greater prophet than John the Baptist; but he that is least in the kingdom of God is greater than he." How is it that John was considered one of the greatest prophets? His miracles could not have constituted his greatness.*
>
> *First. He was entrusted with a divine mission of preparing the way before the face of the Lord. Whoever had such a trust committed to him before or since? No man.*
>
> *Secondly. He was entrusted with the important mission, and it was required at his hands, to baptize the Son of Man. Whoever had the honor of doing that? Whoever had so great a privilege and glory? Whoever led the Son of God into the waters of baptism, and had the privilege of beholding the Holy Ghost descend in the form of a dove, or rather in the* sign *of the dove, in witness of that administration? The sign of the dove was instituted before the creation of the*

world, a witness for the Holy Ghost, and the devil cannot come in the sign of a dove. The Holy Ghost is a personage, and is in the form of a personage. It does not confine itself to the form of the dove, but in sign of the dove. The Holy Ghost cannot be transformed into a dove; but the sign of a dove was given to John to signify the truth of the deed, as the dove is an emblem or token of truth and innocence.

*Thirdly. John, at that time, was the only legal adminis-trator in the affairs of the kingdom there was then on the earth, and holding the keys of power. The Jews had to obey his instructions or be damned, by their own law; and Christ Himself fulfilled all righteousness in becoming obedient to the law which he had given to Moses on the mount, and thereby magnified it and made it honorable, instead of de-stroying it. The son of Zacharias wrested the keys, the king-dom, the power, the glory from the Jews, by the holy anoint-ing and decree of heaven, and these three reasons constitute him the greatest prophet born of a woman. (*Teachings, pp. 275–76.*)*

The great issue in John's day was not whether people needed to be baptized but rather whether John was the rightful heir of Aaron sent to fill the promises made by Isaiah and Malachi rela-tive to the messenger who would be sent to prepare the way for their Messiah. It would miss the point to suppose that the issue was not understood by those involved in the drama. For genera-tions, those holding the office once belonging to Aaron knew that it was but a temporary trust and that the time would come when its legitimate heir would be manifest. (See 1 Maccabees 4:42–46; 14:41.) It was for this reason that the delegation was sent from the temple to Jordan to interrogate John and find out who he claimed to be. Why, they asked him, did he baptize if he did not claim to be the Christ, Elijah, or the prophet who was to come? (See John 1:19–28.) The implication here is clear. The Jews understood that the Messiah and those who attended his coming would bring with them a new baptism.

The dialogue in JST Matthew 9:18–21 illustrates that it is authority and not baptism that was the issue with the Jews.

> *Then said the Pharisees unto him, Why will ye not receive us with our baptism, seeing we keep the whole law?*
>
> *But Jesus said unto them, Ye keep not the law. If ye had kept the law, ye would have received me, for I am he who gave the law.*
>
> *I receive not you with your baptism, because it profiteth you nothing.*
>
> *For when that which is new is come, the old is ready to be put away.*

This Is My Beloved Son, Hear Him

"After John had been testifying of Jesus for some time," Joseph Smith explained, "Jesus came unto him for baptism. John felt that the honor of baptizing his master was too great a thing—greater than he could claim—and said, 'I have need to be baptized of thee, and comest thou to me?' Jesus replied: 'Thus it behooveth us to fulfill all righteousness,' thus signifying to John the claim of the Aaronic Priesthood, which holds the keys of entrance into the kingdom. . . . Jesus . . . could not enter except by the administration of John." (*The Words of Joseph Smith*, p. 66.)

The most instructive account of the baptism of the Savior is found in the Joseph Smith Translation:

> *And then cometh Jesus from Galilee to Jordan, unto John, to be baptized of him;*
>
> *But John refused him, saying, I have need to be baptized of thee, and why comest thou to me?*
>
> *And Jesus, answering, said unto him, Suffer me to be baptized of thee, for thus it becometh us to fulfill all righteousness. Then he suffered him.*
>
> *And John went down into the water and baptized him.*
>
> *And Jesus when he was baptized, went up straightway out of the water; and John saw, and lo, the heavens were*

opened unto him, and he saw the Spirit of God descending like a dove and lighting upon Jesus.

And lo, he heard a voice from heaven, saying, This is my beloved Son, in whom I am well pleased. Hear ye him. (JST Matthew 3:41–46.)

From this account we learn that John saw the heavens open, saw the Holy Ghost descend, and also heard the voice of the Lord testify that Jesus was his Son. Further, the command to "hear" the Lord or give attention to that which he will teach is not directed to John alone but to all who have ears to hear. As noted earlier, the Twelve, with the possible exception of Judas, probably were all present—they too heard the voice of the Father testifying that Jesus of Nazareth was his Son and they too saw the dove descend from heaven as the sign or token of the presence of the Holy Ghost.

A Gospel Written by the Baptist Is to Be Restored to Us

In a revelation given to the Prophet Joseph Smith we learn that John the Baptist left a written testimony of Christ. This revelation restores part of that testimony for us, with the promise that at some future time we will have it in its fulness. That revelation, D&C 93, reads as follows:

And John saw and bore record of the fulness of my glory, and the fulness of John's record is hereafter to be revealed.

And he bore record, saying: I saw his glory, that he was in the beginning, before the world was;

In his Gospel, the Baptist recorded things seen by the spirit of revelation—things that reached back to the pre-earth life.

Therefore, in the beginning the Word was, for he was the Word, even the messenger of salvation—

The light and the Redeemer of the world; the Spirit of

truth, who came into the world, because the world was made
by him, and in him was the life of men and the light of men.
The worlds were made by him; men were made by him;
all things were made by him, and through him, and of him.

Under the direction of the Father, Christ is the creator of all
things; he is their source of light and salvation. Through Adam
all that God created became subject to the Fall; through Christ's
atoning sacrifice he becomes the source of their redemption.

And I, John, bear record that I beheld his glory, as the
glory of the Only Begotten of the Father, full of grace and
truth, even the Spirit of truth, which came and dwelt in the
flesh, and dwelt among us.

John testifies of the glory that was Christ's in the pre-earth
life and of the glory that is Christ's as the "Only Begotten of the
Father." All humankind have claim to God as the Father of their
spirits. Christ alone has the honor of having God as the father of
his mortal body. From this unique inheritance he obtained the
power to both lay down his life and take it up again.

And I, John, saw that he received not of the fulness at
the first, but received grace for grace.
And he received not of the fulness at first, but continued
from grace to grace, until he received a fulness;
And thus he was called the Son of God, because he re-
ceived not of the fulness at the first.

Christ, as Son of God, descended below all things. He surrendered the royal majesty that had been his in order to be born
the helpless infant of the young maiden Mary. His first bed was a
manger in a stable, his last a borrowed tomb. From the days of
Eden it was prophesied that Satan would "bruise his heel," but
that Christ as the seed of Eve would bruise the serpent's head
(Moses 4:21). "Though he were a Son, yet learned he obedience

by the things which he suffered, and being made perfect, he became the author of eternal salvation unto all them that obey him" (Hebrews 5:8–9). Christ obtained the fulness of his Father by going from one grace to a greater grace, in so doing marking a path that all who choose may follow.

> *And I, John, bear record, and lo, the heavens were opened, and the Holy Ghost descended upon him in the form of a dove, and sat upon him, and there came a voice out of heaven saying: This is my beloved Son.*

It was not Jesus alone that heard the voice of God testify of Christ's divine sonship, for those sacred words fell also upon the ears of John. "And John went down into the water and baptized him. And Jesus when he was baptized, went up straightway out of the water; and John saw, and lo, the heavens were opened unto him, and he saw the Spirit of God descending like a dove and lighting upon Jesus. And lo, he heard a voice from heaven, saying, This is my beloved Son, in whom I am well pleased. Hear ye him." (JST Matthew 3:44–46.)

> *And I, John, bear record that he received a fulness of the glory of the Father;*
> *And he received all power, both in heaven and on earth, and the glory of the Father was with him, for he dwelt in him.*

Such is the testimony of him who was filled with the Holy Ghost even from his mother's womb. This passage, like so many others, dispels the mistaken notion that the Father and the Son are of the same essence. Latter-day Saints worship the Father in the name of the Son (see D&C 20:19, 29). Following the example of Christ we seek salvation at the hands of the Father.

> *And it shall come to pass, that if you are faithful you shall receive the fulness of the record of John.*

The time will come when the Gospel written by the Baptist will be restored and be numbered among those scriptural texts enjoyed by those of the household of faith.

The Return of the Baptist in Our Day

The essential purpose of the Aaronic Priesthood is to testify of Christ. It is the priesthood charged to prepare the way before him in both the meridian and the millennial days. In Bible times this priesthood administered the law given at Sinai to prepare for his mortal ministry. Everything, for instance, in the temple ritual was designed to testify of Christ and his great redemptive labor. John, because he held the keys of that priesthood, was commissioned to overthrow the kingdom of the Jews, which had corrupted the divinely instituted order. This he did by preaching faith, repentance, and baptism. The Aaronic Priesthood also included the authority by which the law of sacrifice was administered. It was through shedding the blood of the lamb that the promise of protection from all of the effects of Adam's fall came. Thus we read that "all things were confirmed unto Adam [and his faithful posterity], by an holy ordinance" (Moses 5:59).

When John the Baptist appeared to Joseph Smith and Oliver Cowdery on May 15, 1829, he bestowed upon them the same authority by which he had ministered in the meridian day. He gave them the keys of the ministering of angels, the commission to declare the doctrine of repentance, and the authority to baptize for the remission of sins. He also restored the right by which the sons of Levi offered an acceptable offering to the Lord in that ancient day, that we through that same "holy ordinance" might testify anew of the redeeming blood of God's Son. (See D&C 13.)

It would be difficult to overstate the importance of the restoration of the Aaronic Priesthood. The language in which John began the ordination seems marvelously relevant to the story we tell: "Upon you my fellow servants," he said, "in the name of Messiah. . . ." So it was that he united his labor with theirs as servants of the same master, the very Messiah of whom he had born witness during the days of his mortal ministry. Describing this event, Oliver Cowdery wrote:

> *The Lord, who is rich in mercy, and ever willing to answer the consistent prayer of the humble, after we had called upon Him in a fervent manner, aside from the abodes of men, condescended to manifest to us His will. On a sudden, as from the midst of eternity, the voice of the Redeemer spake peace to us, while the veil was parted and the angel of God came down clothed with glory, and delivered the anxiously looked for message, and the keys of the Gospel of repentance. What joy! what wonder! what amazement! While the world was racked and distracted—while millions were groping as the blind for the wall, and while all men were resting upon uncertainty, as a general mass, our eyes beheld, our ears heard, as in the "blaze of day"; yes, more— above the glitter of the May sunbeam, which then shed its brilliancy over the face of nature! Then his voice, though mild, pierced to the center, and his words, "I am thy fellow- servant," dispelled every fear. We listened, we gazed, we admired! 'Twas the voice of an angel from glory, 'twas a message from the Most High! And as we heard we rejoiced, while His love enkindled upon our souls, and we were wrapped in the vision of the Almighty! Where was room for doubt? Nowhere; uncertainty had fled, doubt had sunk no more to rise, while fiction and deception had fled forever! (Joseph Smith—History 1:71, footnote, fifth paragraph.)*

Significantly, every ordinance and function associated with this priesthood, including baptism, the sacrament of the Lord's supper, and the declaration of the gospel, is done in the name of the Son of God (See D&C 20:73, 77, 79). All that John did he did in the sacred name of the Son of God.

NOTE

1. Regarding this statement, Andrew F. Ehat and Lyndon W. Cook observed: "Because of respect to Zacharias's keys, God sent the angel Gabriel." (*The Words of Joseph Smith,* p. 90.)

CHAPTER FOUR

Handmaidens of the Lord

When Elisabeth heard the salutation of Mary, the babe leaped in her womb

Two women, one young and the other old, each perfect in her generation, now chosen of God to give birth by miracle—if the miracle of birth itself were not enough—to a son of destiny. The name of each child had been announced by the angel of God even as they had been chosen by divine decree to their ministries long before their birth into mortality. The first of them born into this fallen world would bear the name John. He would be the son of the law, or order of Aaron, by which authority he would stand as the culmination of all that the Mosaic system was instituted to do in introducing the Lamb of God to the generation in which he would make the great and last sacrifice.

The second, the Messenger of the Covenant, the manifestation of the grace of God or his condescension, as Nephi would call it, bearing the name Jesus, would bring with him the fulness of all that had been promised to the prophets of old, even the fulfillment of the promises made long ago in the councils of heaven.

Both would be born in humble circumstances, yet in the birth of both the stars of heaven would shout with joy! And in it all we sense the propriety of heaven in having the story of its greatest characters begin with two helpless infants in the arms of loving mothers—the handmaidens of the Lord.

Elisabeth's Reproach to Be Taken Away
(Luke 1:24–25)

And after those days his wife Elisabeth conceived, and
hid herself five months, saying,
    Thus hath the Lord dealt with me in the days wherein
he looked on me, to take away my reproach among men.

We are not told why Elisabeth chose to hide herself for the first five months of her pregnancy. Her doing so did, however, keep the matter secret so that Mary's knowledge of her condition came only from Gabriel. Thus her meeting with Elisabeth served as a confirmation of that which the angel had told her.

As with Sarah so many years before, Elisabeth's conception, long after the normal years of child bearing had passed her, was miraculous. Thus Isaac, through whom the promise of the covenant was preserved, John, who would prepare the way for the Messenger of the Covenant, and Jesus himself were all miraculously conceived. How better, we might ask, to dramatize the miracle of salvation that comes to us through Christ?

The "reproach" felt by the childless woman in Israel is captured in Rachel's plea to her husband, Jacob: "Give me children, or else I die" (Genesis 30:1).

Gabriel Visits Mary
(Luke 1:26–27)

And in the sixth month the angel Gabriel was sent
from God unto a city of Galilee, named Nazareth,
    To a virgin espoused to a man whose name was Joseph,
of the house of David; and the virgin's name was Mary.

Notwithstanding the very humble circumstances of her birth, Mary, the "precious and chosen vessel" of the Lord, laid claim to the two most honored lineages in Israel. She was on the one hand a descendant of the royal line of David and on the other claimed the blood line of Levi, or that of Israel's priests. The fact that both she and Joseph were of the Davidic line, whose patrimonial estates were in Bethlehem, raises the question as to why both families had moved some eighty miles northward from the Holy City and Temple. "It is probable," observes Adam Clarke, "that the holy family removed to Galilee for fear of exciting the jealousy of Herod, who had usurped that throne to which they had an indisputable right" (*The Holy Bible . . . with Commentary and Critical Notes,* 6 vols., Nashville: Abingdon, n.d., 5:359). Their hope was that by keeping out of sight they might avoid his fiendish wrath. It was here in Galilee that Gabriel appeared to Mary.

Mary was espoused to Joseph, meaning she had entered into a contract of marriage with him. This contract would be completed in a second ceremony normally held about a year later. Only after the second ceremony would they begin living together as husband and wife. Nevertheless, by Jewish law Mary was considered to be Joseph's wife at the time of espousal; their contract could be broken only by a formal "letter of divorcement." Any infidelity on her part would be classed as adultery, which from the time of Moses carried the decree of death.

Mary Blessed Among Women
(Luke 1:28)

And the angel came in unto her, and said, Hail, thou that art highly favoured, the Lord is with thee: blessed art thou among women.

In the councils of heaven when all the spirit children of our Eternal Father assembled together, Mary stood prominent among all female spirits. She whom Gabriel called "highly favoured" of God had by virtue of the purity of her soul and her loyalty to principles of truth found a place, like unto him who would be her firstborn son, "in the bosom of the Father" (see D&C 76:25). Her place in history was foreordained. She was the one the Father had chosen to nurture his only child to be born in the flesh. There was no greater honor that the Father of us all could bestow upon any woman. Only Eve, who had been chosen to be the mother of all living and who stood as the prototype of womanhood, could approach her in greatness. Of those born in the flesh there is no woman whom the Saints hold in greater esteem than Mary.

She is honored most perfectly in the virtue and purity of motherhood and in that desire natural to the hearts of women to do the will of God.

Mary Chosen to Be the Mother of God's Son (Luke 1:29–31)

And when she saw him, she was troubled at his saying, and cast in her mind what manner of salutation this should be.

And the angel said unto her, Fear not, Mary: for thou hast found favour with God.

And, behold, thou shalt conceive in thy womb, and bring forth a son, and shalt call his name JESUS.

According to the custom of the day girls were normally betrothed at the age of twelve. It would be natural for one of such humble circumstances and tender years to feel uncomfortable with such high praise. Apparently sensing this, Gabriel assured Mary there was nothing to fear. He then explained that she would conceive a male child who was to bear the name Jesus.

It was imperative that the child bear the right name. *Jesus*, as the name is rendered for us from Greek texts, would be *Joshua* if New Testament manuscripts had been written in Hebrew. This was a common name among the Jews. The name means "Jehovah saves," and properly points to the fact that salvation is in Jesus and in no other.

The Son of the Highest
(Luke 1:32–33)

He shall be great, and shall be called the Son of the Highest: and the Lord God shall give unto him the throne of his father David:

And he shall reign over the house of Jacob for ever; and of his kingdom there shall be no end.

That Jesus was to be "the Son of the Highest" affirms that the Father and Son are separate and distinct personages and that the Father is greater than the Son. "My Father," Christ testified, "is greater than I" (John 14:28). It was from his Father that Christ inherited the power of everlasting life (John 5:26). It is as a son of David, or through Mary, that the Christ child inherited blood or mortality. It is this dual inheritance that enabled Christ to lay down his life in death and take it up again in a resurrected state.

Gabriel told Mary that the child she would bear would inherit the throne of his father David. If Joseph alone had been descended from David, Mary should have answered, "I am not yet married to Joseph," but instead she simply answered "I am an unmarried woman," which implies that if she were married her son would have right by birth to David's throne. The difficulty was not one of descent but that Mary knew not a man.

The Nature of Christ's Conception
(Luke 1:34–35)

Then said Mary unto the angel, How shall this be, seeing I know not a man?

And the angel answered and said unto her, The Holy Ghost shall come upon thee, and the power of the Highest shall overshadow thee: therefore also that holy thing which shall be born of thee shall be called the Son of God.

Every Jewish girl of the lineage of David would know of the promise that one of their number would give birth to their Messiah. We would suppose that each of them had embraced the hope that they might be chosen for such a glorious honor. Mary is here told that not only will her son be King of the Jews but that he also will be the Son of the Everlasting Father.

By way of explanation as to how the child would be conceived Gabriel said, "The Holy Ghost shall come upon thee, and the power of the Highest shall overshadow thee." This text corrects the misimpression created by Matthew, which appears to say that Christ is the child of the Holy Ghost (see Matthew 1:18, 20). In harmony with Luke's declaration, Alma, speaking with the voice of prophecy, said that Mary, a virgin, would "be overshadowed and conceive by the power of the Holy Ghost, and bring forth a son, yea, even the Son of God" (Alma 7:10). Nephi testified that Mary would be the mother of the "Son of God, after the manner of the flesh" (1 Nephi 11:18; see also Acts 2:30; 13:22–23; Romans 1:3).

All the holy prophets since the world began have testified of Christ (see Jacob 4:4, 11; Mosiah 13:33), frequently speaking of him as the "Son of God."

Mary Is Told of Elisabeth's Condition
(Luke 1:36–37)

And, behold, thy cousin Elisabeth, she hath also conceived a son in her old age: and this is the sixth month with her, who was called barren.

For with God nothing shall be impossible.

Scholars tell us that the word *cousin* in this text would more properly have been translated *relative*, suggesting some uncertainty as to exactly what the family tie between Mary and Elisabeth was. It was John Wycliff who put *cousin* into the English text. For Gabriel not to be able to use a more explicit term than *relative* makes him appear both distant and uninformed. That could hardly be the case. The story assumes that a closeness already exists between the two women, notwithstanding the miles that separated them at that time.

Gabriel's announcement about Elisabeth was unspoken counsel to Mary to go and receive comfort and help from her. Mary undoubtedly loved and revered Elisabeth. The inference is that Mary's own mother was dead and that Elisabeth (perhaps her mother's sister) would be a mother to her. Finding Elisabeth with child would also be a confirmation for Mary of all that the angel had told her.

When promising a child to Sarah, Jehovah asked: "Is any thing too hard for the LORD?" (Genesis 18:14.) In a similar spirit Gabriel said, "For with God nothing shall be impossible."

Mary Accepts the Will of God
(Luke 1:38–39)

> *And Mary said, Behold the handmaid of the Lord; be it unto me according to thy word. And the angel departed from her.*
>
> *And Mary arose in those days, and went into the hill country with haste, into a city of Juda;*

Commenting on the spirit of Mary's answer, Elder McConkie wrote, "Then Mary gave the answer that ranks, in submissive obedience and divine conformity, along with the one given by the Beloved and Chosen One in the councils of eternity. When he was chosen to be the Redeemer and to put into operation the terms and conditions of his Father's plan he said: 'Father, thy will be done, and the glory be thine forever.' (Moses 4:2.) Mary said simply: 'Behold the handmaid of the Lord; be it unto me according to thy word.'" (*The Mortal Messiah,* 1:319–20.)

Having so spoken, Mary contented herself until the conception had come to pass, and then in haste she went to visit Elisabeth, who it appears lived in Hebron of Judea, a distance of something near one hundred and twenty miles from Nazareth.

Mary, of course, could not have gone alone. In that day one could join a company for the purpose of safety in traveling. Still it is doubtful that Mary would have gone with a company of strangers without a friend or relative at her side to look after her.

The Testimonies of Mary and Elisabeth
(Luke 1:40–41)

And entered into the house of Zacharias, and saluted Elisabeth.

And it came to pass, that, when Elisabeth heard the salutation of Mary, the babe leaped in her womb; and Elisabeth was filled with the Holy Ghost:

The appearance of Mary is a joyful surprise to Elisabeth. Her condition could only have been conveyed to Mary by an angel. No one but Elisabeth and her speechless husband knew of it; that is, none but the angel of the Lord, who had spoken her name to Mary. Both women are filled with the deepest of emotion and with the Holy Ghost, whose presence is common to such occasions and feelings. Their hearts are one. Their faith is one. The bond between them now reaches well beyond the ties that had previously bound them together.

We can but suppose that Elisabeth knows full well what rights belong to her son by birth as the rightful heir of Aaron's seat if her nation were not in a state of apostasy. She also knows of the kingly lineage that belongs to Mary's family. She cannot be unmindful of the danger that this represents.

John, who has been promised the Holy Ghost even in his mother's womb, leaps in recognition of Mary and her unborn child.

Elisabeth's Psalm of Praise
(Luke 1:42–45)

And she spake out with a loud voice, and said, Blessed art thou among women, and blessed is the fruit of thy womb.

*And whence is this to me, that the mother of my Lord
should come to me?*
*For, lo, as soon as the voice of thy salutation sounded in
mine ears, the babe leaped in my womb for joy.*
*And blessed is she that believed: for there shall be a per-
formance of those things which were told her from the Lord.*

Elisabeth greets Mary in the spirit of prophecy. Her testimony embraces the fact that Mary, though not noticeably pregnant, already carries the Son of God in her womb. The meeting
serves as a confirmation to both women of the promises made to
them by Gabriel. No longer need they stand alone. They will be
a great comfort to each other. Each expresses her joy with a can-
ticle of praise.

Mary's Psalm of Praise
(Luke 1:46–48)

And Mary said, My soul doth magnify the Lord,
And my spirit hath rejoiced in God my Saviour.
For he hath regarded the low estate of his handmaiden:
*for, behold, from henceforth all generations shall call me
blessed.*

These prophetic words spoken by Mary constitute a remarkable prophecy. The time was about 6 B.C.; the place, an obscure
village in the province of Galilee. The speaker, a girl perhaps in
her early teens, one of no social standing, and having no claim to
fortune. Yet the prophecy is that her name will be had in honorable remembrance by all generations that follow. We know of but
one other prophecy that can match this in its improbability and its
audacity, that being the prophetic words spoken by the angel Moroni to the youthful Joseph Smith, wherein he was told that his
name would be known for both good and evil among those of
every nation, kindred, tongue, and people (see Joseph Smith—
History 1:33). Joseph's situation in life was equally obscure with

that of Mary, and the possibility of this prophecy being fulfilled was at the time equally unlikely.

In this psalm we are assured that Mary "rejoiced in God [her] Saviour," thus assuring us that she, like all who have descended from Adam, is in need of a Savior.

Mary Testifies of the Goodness of God
(Luke 1:49–55)

For he that is mighty hath done to me great things; and holy is his name.

And his mercy is on them that fear him from generation to generation.

He hath shewed strength with his arm; he hath scattered the proud in the imagination of their hearts.

He hath put down the mighty from their seats, and exalted them of low degree.

He hath filled the hungry with good things; and the rich he hath sent empty away.

He hath holpen [helped] his servant Israel, in remembrance of his mercy;

As he spake to our fathers, to Abraham, and to his seed for ever.

As the mother of the Son of God, Mary has received the greatest honor ever bestowed upon a mortal woman. Her testimony is of God's power and goodness. In the birth of his Son, both promise and covenant made to Abraham and his seed will find fulfillment.

Mary Returns to Nazareth
(Luke 1:56)

And Mary abode with her about three months, and returned to her own house.

We can but think that Joseph, having had the heavens opened to him, now sends for Mary that he might take her as his wife.

Elisabeth Gives Birth to John
(Luke 1:57–58)

Now Elisabeth's full time came that she should be delivered; and she brought forth a son.

And her neighbours and her cousins [relatives] heard how the Lord had shewed great mercy upon her; and they rejoiced with her.

It was just prior to these events that Mary departed, perhaps to avoid causing embarrassment, for she would now be noticeably pregnant and yet unmarried. We only suppose that the two mothers made promises that would bring them and their sons together again. Such meetings would probably center around the religious holidays that would bring devout Jews to the temple at set times each year.

The Birth of the Christ Child
(Luke 2:1–5)

And it came to pass in those days, that there went out a decree from Caesar Augustus, that all the world should be taxed.

(And this taxing was first made when Cyrenius was governor of Syria.)

And all went to be taxed, every one into his own city.

And Joseph also went up from Galilee, out of the city of Nazareth, into Judaea, unto the city of David, which is called Bethlehem; (because he was of the house and lineage of David:)

To be taxed with Mary his espoused wife, being great with child.

It was not the payment of taxes that brought Joseph and Mary from Nazareth to Bethlehem. Nor did Caesar Augustus[1] have the power to tax "all the world." His authority to tax rested only with the Roman Empire.[2] What was required by Caesar Augustus was a census. Had Judea been, as she would yet become, a mere Roman province, her census would have been taken after the Roman method; since she was still a kingdom, it was taken after the Jewish method, which required each person to repair to his ancestral seat to be recorded. It could hardly be supposed that the Jewish system would require one in Mary's delicate state to travel from Nazareth to Bethlehem. Mary and Joseph came from Nazareth to Bethlehem because they knew that in the providence of heaven the Christ child was to be born in Bethlehem, which was the original family home for them both.

In following the terrain one does not "go up from Galilee" to the city of David or Bethlehem. The better part of the journey of some ninety miles would be down the Jordan River Valley to Jericho. Only after leaving Jericho would one ascend to the Mountain of the Lord. Bethlehem, or the city of David, was nestled in the hills about four or five miles south of the Holy City. Its proximity was such that New World prophets simply spoke of it as Jerusalem (see Alma 7:10). The Holy City with its temple was built upon a hill; thus, regardless of the direction from which the faithful came, they ascended the hill of the Lord in both a physical and a spiritual sense.

Bethlehem, meaning "house of bread," was the city of David's birth and the place where he was anointed Israel's king (see 1 Samuel 16:13). According to prophecy it was to be the place of the Messiah's birth (see Micah 5:2).

Mary was no longer Joseph's "espoused," meaning "promised," wife. Joseph had taken her as wife in proper ceremony. Were this not the case it would have been quite improper for them to travel together to Bethlehem.

The Birth of Christ
(Luke 2:6–7)

And so it was, that, while they were there, the days were accomplished that she should be delivered.

And she brought forth her firstborn son, and wrapped him in swaddling clothes, and laid him in a manger; because there was no room for them in the inn.

Hospitality to the traveler was very much the custom of the Jewish people. This would be particularly so in Jerusalem and the surrounding area during religious holy days. That Joseph and Mary sought lodging in an inn suggests either that they had no relatives or friends in Bethlehem or that they sought privacy for the birth of the child. Though the village was crowded, surely room would have been made somewhere for family—particulary considering Mary's condition. Such an arrangment, however, would have been in a small private house consisting of a single room already crowded with visitors.

The often quoted statement that "there was no room for them in the inn" can be read to say that there may have been room for others, but not for them. In the JST Joseph Smith rendered the text "inns," which strengthens that suspicion.

The typical inn or caravansary in the ancient Near East consisted of a four-sided structure with separate rooms around its inner walls. These rooms faced an open court where the animals used in travel were kept. Sometimes the inns were built out from a cave so that even the animals would have a place of shelter if the weather was bad.

Of these rooms, Farrar says:

They are, of course, perfectly public; everything that takes place in them is visible to every person in the kahn. They are also totally devoid of even the most ordinary furniture. The traveller may bring his own carpet if he likes, may sit cross-legged upon it for his meals, and may lie upon it at night.

As a rule, too, he must bring his own food, attend to his own cattle, and draw his own water from the neighbouring spring. He would neither expect nor require attendance, and would pay only the merest trifle for the advantage of shelter, safety, and a floor on which to lie. But if he chanced to arrive late, and the leewans [rooms] were all occupied by earlier guests, he would have no choice but to be content with such accommodation as he could find in the court-yard below, and secure for himself and his family such small amount of cleanliness and decency as are compatible with an unoccupied corner on the filthy area, which must be shared with horses, mules, and camels. The litter, the close-ness, the unpleasant smell of the crowded animals, the un-welcome intrusion of the pariah dogs, the necessary society of the very lowest hangers-on of the caravansary, are adjuncts to such a position which can only be realized by any traveller in the East who happens to have been placed in similar cir-cumstances." (Frederic W. Farrar, The Life of Christ, *Portland: Fountain Publications, 1964, pp. 33–34.)*

The distinctive sign given to the shepherds by which they were to identify the Christ child was the manger, not the swaddling clothes. To place a child in a manger or cattle trough is highly un-usual. Swaddling clothes, on the other hand, were simply strips of cloth in which the child was wrapped. This was the traditional way to care for the newborn and was a sign of parental care. That Mary wrapped the child is taken by some as evidence that she was without help in giving birth to the child.

To describe Christ as Mary's "firstborn son" is at the same time to suggest that other children were born to Mary and Joseph. As previously noted, Mary was the mother of both sons and daughters (see Matthew 13:55–56; Mark 6:3).

The Testimony of Two Women

Elisabeth and Mary were, as our story tells us, kinswomen. Precisely what their relationship was, we do not know. Along with a common bloodline, they shared the same devotion to the law given their people by Jehovah on Sinai and the blessings associated with being of humble circumstance. Elisabeth was the daughter of a priest and the wife of another. Mary was a descendant of the royal line of David. Appropriately these two women, one old and the other young, stand among the first of the meridian witnesses of the birth of God's Son.

NOTES

1. David Smith, *The Days of His Flesh* (Grand Rapids, Michigan, 1976), p. 3.

2. Caesar Augustus ruled from 27 B.C. to A.D. 14. Secular sources provide no evidence of any census being conducted in "all the world"—a hyperbole for the Roman Empire—during his reign. An enrollment in the province of Syria for purposes of taxation was undertaken in A.D. 6 or 7 when Quirinius was governor. This would have been at least ten years after the death of Herod. It may be that Luke was simply given misinformation on this matter.

CHAPTER FIVE

The Shepherds

Shepherds tending the temple flock became the first witnesses of Christ's birth

To whom, we might ask, should the announcement first be made that the King of the Jews had been born? Should those "glad tidings of great joy" be announced first in the court of King Herod, the cruel and wicked tyrant who wrongfully held that office? Or should the announcement of the birth of the Savior of all mankind have been made first in the throne room of the mighty Caesar Augustus, himself heralded as a god? Or should it have been made to the presiding high priest of the temple—the Caiaphas of that day? Or among the Pharisees, who so zealously protected the law and then used it as the excuse to reject the Christ? Or what of the Sadducees, who despite their hatred of the Pharisees would join hands with them in seeking the blood of Christ; should it have gone first to them? And what of the Essenes, who cursed their enemies and awaited the day of their power in their desert refuge at Qumran—was it for *them* to entertain angels?

How perfect the wisdom of heaven that such an announcement be made first to those who best understood the responsibility of tending the Lord's flock!

An Angelic Choir Sings to Humble Shepherds
(Luke 2:8–14)

And there were in the same country shepherds abiding in the field, keeping watch over their flock by night.

And, lo, the angel of the Lord came upon them, and the glory of the Lord shone around about them: and they were sore afraid.

And the angel said unto them, Fear not: for, behold, I bring you good tidings of great joy, which shall be to all people.

For unto you is born this day in the city of David a Saviour, which is Christ the Lord.

And this shall be a sign unto you; Ye shall find the babe wrapped in swaddling clothes, lying in a manger.

And suddenly there was with the angel a multitude of the heavenly host praising God, and saying,

Glory to God in the highest, and on earth peace, good will toward men.

And who were these men destined to be the first earthly witnesses of the birth of Christ? They were simple shepherds, but not ordinary shepherds by any means. "It seems of deepest significance," writes Alfred Edersheim, . . . "that those shepherds who first heard tidings of the Saviour's birth, who first listened to angels' praises, were watching flocks destined to be offered as sacrifices in the Temple." Near Bethlehem on the road to Jerusalem was a tower known as *Migdal Eder,* the "watch-tower of the flock." It was here that shepherds tended the flocks destined for sacrifices in the house of the Lord. In that ancient day this area was sufficiently well known that if animals wandered from Jerusalem and were found in it they too would be used as Temple offerings—male animals as burnt-offerings, females as peace-offerings. (Alfred Edersheim, *Sketches of Jewish Social Life,* Hendrickson Publishers, 1994, pp. 76–77.)

We are tempted to wonder whether those same shepherds were descendants of Aaron, and thus by birth rightful heirs of that priesthood which bore his name and by office charged with the responsibility to announce the coming of their Messiah and to prepare the way before him.[1]

The well-known line in the King James Version, "Glory to God in the highest, and on earth peace, good will toward men," sung by the angelic choir to the shepherds, though not a mistranslation is not the best of translations either. More properly it could read, "Glory to God in the highest heaven," while qualifying the promise of peace "to men of good will," or with whom "he [God] is pleased." We can confidently say that it was to shepherds with whom the Lord was well pleased that his heavenly choir was sent.

Shepherds: The Perfect Metaphor

It seems most fitting that the birth of the Messiah, whose ministry had so often been foreshadowed as that of the Good Shepherd, would be announced by those in whose image he came. By day or night a good shepherd would always be found with his sheep. With the rising of the sun in the morning, if his sheep were sharing a communal fold he would call them forth, each shepherd in turn doing so by name (see John 10:3–4). It was for him to lead them to pasture and fresh water (Psalm 23). In the lands of the Bible, today as anciently, the shepherd will be found leading his sheep rather than driving them (see John 10:4). It is his duty to protect the flock from wild animals (see 1 Samuel 17:34–35) and robbers (see John 10:1). While they graze he will call them from time to time to assure them that he is near. While the sheep hear his voice they continue grazing, but should they instead hear the voice of another they become startled and begin to scatter. Should a sheep stray, the shepherd will search until it is found (see Luke 15:4). As the sun begins to set, the good shepherd will lead his sheep to a place of shelter and protection, either a fold or a natural enclosure, where he will assure himself that none have been lost (see Jeremiah 33:13).

A commentator on traditions in the Bible lands observes:

The shepherd comes to know his sheep very intimately. Many of them have pet names suggested either by the appearance or character of the particular sheep, or by some incident connected with it. At sunset the sheep are counted, usually two by two; but as a rule when they are brought together, the absence of any one is immediately felt. It is not only that one sheep is missing, but the appearance of the whole flock seems to want something. This knowledge is so intimate and instinctively reliable that the formality of counting is often dispensed with. One day a missionary, meeting a shepherd on one of the wildest parts of the Lebanon, asked him various questions about his sheep, and among others if he counted them every night. On answering that he did not, he was asked how he knew if they were all there or not. His reply was, "Master, if you were to put a cloth over my eyes, and bring me any sheep and only let me put my hands on its face, I could tell in a moment if it was mine or not." Such is the fulness of meaning in the words of the Good Shepherd, "I know mine own, and mine own know Me" (John 10:14). (George M. Mackie, Bible Manners and Customs, *Fleming H. Revell Company, n.d., p. 35.)*

How natural the likeness between those who tended the Lord's flock and our Lord himself, of whom Paul spoke as "that great shepherd of the sheep" (Hebrews 13:20). Surely it is not without significance that the progenitors of their race in the patriarchal age to which their Messianic hopes are traced were themselves shepherds. David, who elicited the promise of the Lord that the Messiah would be of his lineage, was himself a shepherd tending his father's flocks in these same fields and he too was born in Bethlehem—which the angels who sang to the shepherds identified as the city of David.

Indeed, the term *shepherd* is applied in metaphor to princes (Jeremiah 2:8), prophets (Zechariah 11:5), teachers (Ecclesiastes 12:11), and all who go forth in the name of the "great shepherd" (Psalm 23). Thus Alma wrote:

O ye workers of iniquity; ye that are puffed up in the vain things of the world, ye that have professed to have known the ways of righteousness nevertheless have gone astray, as sheep having no shepherd, notwithstanding a shepherd hath called after you and is still calling after you, but ye will not hearken unto his voice!

Behold, I say unto you that the good shepherd doth call you; yea, and in his own name he doth call you, which is the name of Christ; and if ye will not hearken unto the voice of the good shepherd, to the name by which ye are called, behold, ye are not the sheep of the good shepherd.

And now if ye are not the sheep of the good shepherd, of what fold are ye? Behold, I say unto you, that the devil is your shepherd, and ye are of his fold; and now, who can deny this? Behold, I say unto you, whosoever denieth this is a liar and a child of the devil. (Alma 5:37–39.)

And again:

For what shepherd is there among you having many sheep doth not watch over them, that the wolves enter not and devour his flock? And behold, if a wolf enter his flock doth he not drive him out? Yea, and at the last, if he can, he will destroy him.

And now I say unto you that the good shepherd doth call after you; and if you will hearken unto his voice he will bring you into his fold, and ye are his sheep; and he commandeth you that ye suffer no ravenous wolf to enter among you, that ye may not be destroyed. (Alma 5:59–60.)

Just and Holy Men

We can be assured that the angelic choir spoken of by Luke did not appear to all shepherds, but to certain shepherds—shepherds who perhaps were ordained in the councils of heaven to be the first earthly witnesses of the birth of Christ. "These were humble men who had not lost the faith of their fathers, whose hearts had not become hardened as were the hearts of the rulers of the Jews in the days of our Lord's ministry" (Joseph Fielding Smith, *The Restoration of All Things*, Salt Lake City: Deseret Book Co., 1945, p. 279), but who had lived worthy of the companionship of angels. They, like their New World counterparts to whom angels were appearing declaring the same message, were "just and holy men" (Alma 13:26). To be "just" or justified was to stand approved by the law given by Jehovah to Israel. To be "holy" meant that they had separated themselves from sin and that their lives were consecrated to God.

"These were not ordinary shepherds nor ordinary flocks," wrote Elder Bruce R. McConkie.

> *The sheep there being herded—nay, not herded, but watched over, cared for with love and devotion—were destined for sacrifice on the great altar in the Lord's House, in similitude of the eternal sacrifice of Him who that wondrous night lay in a stable, perhaps among sheep of lesser destiny. And the shepherds—for whom the veil was then rent: surely they were in spiritual stature like Simeon and Anna and Zacharias and Elisabeth and Joseph and the growing group of believing souls who were coming to know, by revelation, that the Lord's Christ was now on earth. As there were many widows in Israel, and only to the one in Zarephath was Elijah sent, so there were many shepherds in Palestine, but only to those who watched over the temple flocks did the herald angel come; only they heard the heavenly choir. As Luke's idyllic language has it: "And, lo, the angel of the Lord came upon them, and the glory of the Lord shone round about them: and they were sore afraid." (The Mortal Messiah, 1:347.)*

Shepherds Visit the Christ Child
(Luke 2:15–16)

And it came to pass, as the angels were gone away from them into heaven, the shepherds said one to another, Let us now go even unto Bethlehem, and see this thing which is come to pass, which the Lord hath made known unto us.

And they came with haste, and found Mary, and Joseph, and the babe lying in a manger.

Micah (5:2) prophesied that Bethlehem would become the birthplace of the Messiah. The name Bethlehem means "house of bread" or "house of food," perhaps because of the rich fields east of the town where sheep grazed and wheat and barley grew.

If the place of Christ's birth was known by prophecy many generations before—and people are more important than places—what of those who would be chosen to testify of that event? Would we not suppose that they too were known to God even before the foundations of the earth were laid?

Luke tells us that the shepherds found Jesus, as the angel said they would, lying in a manger wrapped in swaddling clothes. "This was an ancient form of clothing for newborn infants. Sometimes this was called a 'swaddling band.' It was a square piece of cloth on which the infant was laid with its head at one of the four corners and its feet at the opposite corner. The corner at the head was tucked under the head, and the one at the feet was folded over the feet. The other two corners were folded together over the midsection, then the whole thing was wrapped with bands of cloth." (V. Gilbert Beers, *The Victor Handbook of Bible Knowledge,* Wheaton, Illinois: Victor Books, 1981, p. 326.)

The new-born baby was washed and rubbed over with salt. Not only was this an antiseptic, but it was thought it would make the skin firm. Then it was that the child was snugly wrapped in "swaddling clothes." This would keep the baby's arms and legs straight to assure that they would grow that way.

The Shepherds Call to Scattered Sheep of Israel
(Luke 2:17–20)

And when they had seen it, they made known abroad the saying which was told them concerning this child.

And all they that heard it wondered at those things which were told them by the shepherds.

But Mary kept all these things, and pondered them in her heart.

And the shepherds returned, glorifying and praising God for all the things that they had heard and seen, as it was told unto them.

Said our friend Edersheim:

It is when we remember that presently these shepherds would be in the Temple, and meet those who came thither to worship and to sacrifice, that we perceive the full significance of what otherwise would have seemed scarcely worth while noticing in connection with humble shepherds: "And when they had seen it, they made known abroad the saying which was told them concerning this child. And all they that heard it wondered at those things which were told them by the shepherds" (Luke 2:17, 18). Moreover, we can understand the wonderful impression made on those in the courts of the Temple, as, while they selected their sacrifices, the shepherds told the devout of the speedy fulfillment of all these types in what they had themselves seen and heard in that night of wonders; how eager, curious crowds might gather around to discuss, to wonder, perhaps to mock. . . . Thus the shepherds would be the most effectual heralds of the Messiah in the Temple. (Sketches of Jewish Social Life, pp. 77–78.)

We read that Mary pondered in her heart all that had happened. Could we not suppose that Joseph would do likewise? As the infant child Jesus was destined to grow in wisdom, stature, and favor with God, advancing from grace to grace until that glorious day when he received the fulness of his Father, so it would be with Mary and Joseph also. They too, with the passage of time, would grow in grace and understanding, growing up into an understanding of that which they had experienced.

We are further told that when the shepherds returned from having noised these things abroad they came "glorifying and praising God for all the things that they had heard and seen, as it was told unto them" (Luke 2:20). Edersheim observes that the term *diagnorizo* rendered "make known abroad" appears to be broader than their communication with Joseph, Mary, and any they may have met at night in "the field." He concludes that "after bringing their flocks to the Temple, they would return to their own homes, and carry with them, joyfully and gratefully, tidings of the great salvation." (*Sketches of Jewish Social Life,* p. 78 n.) This he takes as an additional evidence that theirs were the temple flocks. In any event, of this we are certain: the testimony they bore was not confined to the night of our Savior's birth, for such was their experience that they were destined to be lifetime witnesses of his birth.

NOTE

1. Raymond E. Brown in his extensive work *The Birth of the Messiah* (New York: Doubleday, 1993) observes: "We are told that animals found between Jerusalem and Migdal Eder (near Bethlehem) were used for Temple sacrifice, and this tradition has been invoked as support for the idea that the Lucan shepherds in the region near Bethlehem were especially sacred shepherds" (p. 421).

"The Mishnah, the traditional Jewish doctrine collected before the third century A.D. suggests that these were not ordinary shepherds and their sheep. They were shepherds appointed to care for the temple flocks, destined for sacrifices. These flocks stayed in the fields throughout the year, even during the winter.

"The Messiah, whose birth was announced to these shepherds, would someday die at the time of the three o'clock afternoon sacrifice, making it no longer necessary for sheep such as theirs to die for people's sins. The Lamb of God had come to die once and for all, so that lambs such as these would not need to die again. No wonder the angel announced the birth of the Messiah to these shepherds!" (V. Gilbert Beers, *The Victor Handbook of Bible Knowledge,* p. 325.)

CHAPTER SIX

Witnesses in the Temple

"And Simeon blessed them,
and said unto Mary his mother,
Behold this child is set for the fall and rising again
of many in Israel."

For the faithful of Jesus' day the temple was the focal point of worship. Within its sacred portals the devout who could attend united daily in a prayerful plea for the coming of their long-promised Messiah. Here they sought both a national and a personal cleansing and atonement that they might be worthy to receive him. All temple ritual pointed to Christ and was thus a prophecy of both his coming and his ministry. Nor were its rituals confined to the law of Moses alone. The law of sacrifice, for instance, traces all the way back to the Garden of Eden. Given that all temple rituals, and for that matter all gospel ordinances, were a type and a shadow that were to testify of Christ, one could only expect that the announcement of his birth must be heard in the temple also. In this anticipation we are not to be disappointed.

As we have already seen, it was the temple, more particularly the Court of Priests, to which Gabriel came to announce the coming birth of the Messiah. That announcement was made to Zacharias, he being the legal heir of the temple priesthood and thus the rightful voice to announce and prepare the way before the Lord. Such was the inheritance that he would give his son, John.

Shekels of the sanctuary

Having paid homage to the Christ child, presumably it was to the temple that the shepherds, who had learned of his birth from the angelic hosts, repaired to herald their testimony. To those stories we now add that of the coming of the Holy Family to conform with its ritual and the testimonies of the aged patriarch Simeon and the even more venerable Anna.

Christ and the Abrahamic Covenant
(Luke 2:21)

And when eight days were accomplished for the circumcising of the child, his name was called JESUS, which was so named of the angel, before he was conceived in the womb.

From the time of Abraham to that of Christ, circumcision was the token or sign of the Abrahamic covenant. It was the assurance to those of the chosen lineage of the coming of a Messiah. (See Genesis 17:9–14.) According to the tradition of the Jews, had Jesus not been circumcised he could not have been permitted to enter either synagogue or temple, nor would any Jew have listened to him preach or have conversation with him. (See *Clarke's Commentary,* 1:374.)

Circumcision and the naming of the newborn were to take place on the eighth day after birth. As was the case with John, it was a time of solemnity and rejoicing. Relatives and neighbors were always invited to be a part of the event. When Jesus was circumcised it is quite possible that "Zacharias and Elisabeth were there with their new son John" (*The Victor Handbook of Bible Knowledge,* p. 328).

The ceremony could be done at home or in the temple. Given that Joseph and Mary were without a home, perhaps it was done in the temple or even at the home of Zacharias and Elisabeth. In this ritual the child became an heir of the covenant God had made with Israel. It was expected that he would be raised according to the law. In this ceremony the father acted as a sort of high priest, offering his child to God with love and gratitude. The one performing the circumcision said, we are told, words to this effect: "Blessed be the Lord our God, who has sanctified us by His precepts, and given us circumcision." The father of the child was then to respond: "Who has sanctified us by His precepts, and has granted us to introduce our child into the covenant of Abraham our father." (Fred H. Wight, *Manners and Customs of Bible Lands,* Chicago: Moody Press, 1953, p. 109.)

The Ordinances of the House of the Lord
(Luke 2:22–24)

And when the days of her purification according to the law of Moses were accomplished, they brought him to Jerusalem, to present him to the Lord;

(As it is written in the law of the Lord, Every male that openeth the womb shall be called holy to the Lord;)

And to offer a sacrifice according to that which is said in the law of the Lord, A pair of turtledoves, or two young pigeons.

As a Jewish mother, Mary was considered unclean for seven days after the birth of her child and was then expected to remain in isolation for another thirty-three days before she could present herself in the temple (see Leviticus 12:2–4). In the case of a female child an eighty-day purification period was required. It was the issue that came forth from the body that rendered a woman ritually unclean, not the act of conception.

It was for the purpose of this act of purification that Mary came to the temple on the fourty-first day after the birth of her son. The requirement of the law was that she offer "a lamb for a burnt offering (that is, a sacrifice of service and devotion, of worship and self-surrender to the Lord) and also the offering of a turtledove or young pigeon as a sin offering (that is, as its name implies, a sacrifice for the remission of personal sins that had been committed through ignorance). Those too poor to pay for a lamb—and such was the case with Mary—could substitute

another turtledove or young pigeon." (*The Mortal Messiah,*
1:353.) In the performance of this ritual it was not necessary for
the mother to bring her child with her to the temple. This was
usually done, however, with the thought of presenting the child
to God to invoke the blessings of heaven upon him.

If the child was its mother's firstborn and was male, then according to the law it belonged to the Lord. Be it remembered
that when Jehovah slew the firstborn in all the homes of Egypt,
from the firstborn of Pharaoh to the firstborn of the captive in
the dungeon and even the firstborn of all cattle, he saved alive
the firstborn in every family in Israel, on whose door the saving
blood had been sprinkled (see Exodus 12:29). That his goodness
might be remembered to all generations, he took as payment the
firstborn of all the Israelites. These were to be his ministers;
when the sacrificial rites and other holy ordinances were performed, it would be the firstborn in every family who would
minister them. Had this provision remained in force, Jesus would
have been, like Zacharias, a priest in the temple. Such priestly duties, however, were restricted to the tribe of Levi as a reward for
their valiant devotion. Thus the firstborn child was relieved from
such duties by the payment of a redemption tax. (See Exodus 13.)
While in the temple, Joseph and Mary paid that redemption tax
according to the law. "Neither mother nor child was considered
as in the Lord's covenant, or under the Divine protection, till
these ceremonies, prescribed by the law, had been performed"
(*Clarke's Commentary,* 1:373.)

The earliest manuscripts do not refer to Mary's purification
but rather to "their" purification, meaning the purification of
both Mary and Joseph. Translators have made the change from
"their" to "her" so that the Gospel of Luke would accord with
tradition and with the Old Testament as we have it.

Wherein Luke says that "every male that openeth the
womb," a proper rendering of the text would be "firstborn
male" (Exodus 13:12).

The Witness of Simeon
(Luke 2:25–26)

And, behold, there was a man in Jerusalem, whose name was Simeon; and the same man was just and devout, waiting for the consolation of Israel: and the Holy Ghost was upon him.

And it was revealed unto him by the Holy Ghost, that he should not see death, before he had seen the Lord's Christ.

The grand old man Simeon is to be numbered among the faithful who awaited for the fulfillment of the prophets in the birth of a Messiah. Christ was the "consolation of Israel," for in him was to be found their redemption and the fulfillment of all promises given them of God.

Simeon Becomes a Special Witness
(Luke 2:27)

And he came by the Spirit into the temple: and when the parents brought in the child Jesus, to do for him after the custom of the law,

The journey from Bethlehem to the temple would take a little over two hours. It is most likely that Joseph and Mary entered the temple through the so-called Huldah gates in the southern wall. "The Talmud tells us that those who entered the Temple Mount, like Moses on Mount Sinai, removed their shoes, and Josephus tells us that many people dressed in a white garment. In addition, all of the Israelites had to present themselves before the Lord in a state of ethical and ritual purity. There was a bathhouse positioned just outside the southern gates at which Israelite men and women symbolically purified themselves by immersing themselves in a ritual bath before ascending to the Temple Mount." (Richard N. Holzapfel and David R. Seely, *My Father's House*, Salt Lake City: Bookcraft, 1994, p. 57.)

The layout of the temple consisted of progressively more re-strictive courtyards representing a ritual assent to the presence of the Lord. The outermost court, known as the Court of the Gen-tiles, was open to all—only women during menstruation were re-fused admission here. Then came the Court of the Women, to which all Jews were admitted. The third court, or Court of Is-rael, was restricted to male Jews who were ritually clean. Then came the fourth court or holy place to which only priests robed in their priestly vestment were admitted. Finally came the Holy of Holies, which only the high priest could enter and that on Yom Kippur or the Day of Atonement only.

Having entered the Court of the Gentiles, Joseph and Mary would buy themselves two pigeons from the temple authorities, who had a monopoly on the sale of animals used in the sacrifices. Then passing through the east gate they would enter the Court of the Women. Here a stone inscription written in both Latin and Greek forbade non-Jews entrance on pain of death. Here also Joseph and Mary would assure the Levite on duty that they were pure. From this court women could view the sacrifices being made at the altar and receive the priestly benediction that was pronounced from stairs at the doorway of the temple. "In this court the Israelites, both men and women, could pray and sing hymns. The men could enter the court of the temple itself and could stand just inside the gate to witness the sacred ordi-nances being performed. A line in the pavement marked the end of the Court of the Israelites and the beginning of the Court of the Priests, which surrounded the temple." (*My Father's House,* p. 57.) Only priests and Levites could go beyond this point.

"At some point, probably at the inner wall, they would have separated, Mary and Jesus staying in the Court of the Women, and Joseph walking straight through the first eastern gate by going up a low flight of steps through the gate itself (called the Beautiful Gate because of its elaborate decorations). Near the en-trance to the Court of the Women, Mary would have found a Levite and given him her birds, explaining that they were a sin offering for childbirth. She would have then entered and gone upstairs into a gallery to watch while the Levite found a priest, who then sacrificed the two birds." (*My Father's House,* p. 87.)

At some point during this ritual, Joseph and Mary met Simeon.

Simeon Blesses the Christ Child
(Luke 2:28–32)

Then took he him up in his arms, and blessed God, and said,

Lord, now lettest thou thy servant depart in peace, according to thy word:

For mine eyes have seen thy salvation,

Which thou hast prepared before the face of all people;

A light to lighten the Gentiles, and the glory of thy people Israel.

The old man then took the child in his arms and gave him a blessing. Only a fragment of the blessing given has been preserved for us. "Mine eyes," he said, "have seen thy salvation," meaning that God will triumph—that through Christ we can overcome the world and the effects of Adam's fall. The breadth of his blessing is seen in the promise that the victory of the Messiah is not for the Jews alone but for all of God's children. Such had been the promise of Isaiah centuries before (see Isaiah 42:6; 49:6). Had this event been witnessed by any Pharisees, Simeon's reference to the Messiah being "a light to the Gentiles" would have evoked considerable hostility.

A Prophecy of Mary's Sorrow
(Luke 2:33–35)

And Joseph and his mother marveled at those things which were spoken of him.

And Simeon blessed them, and said unto Mary his mother, Behold, this child is set for the fall and rising again

of many in Israel; and for a sign which shall be spoken
against;
     (Yea, a sword shall pierce through thy own soul also,)
that the thoughts of many hearts may be revealed.

Simeon foresaw that Christ and his message would divide the
house of Israel. Similarly, Nephi prophesied saying: "Yea, behold
the house of Israel hath gathered together to fight against the
twelve apostles of the Lamb" (1 Nephi 11:35). Isaiah had prophesied that when the stone of Israel came he would be a sanctuary
for the righteous who would find peace and safety in his teachings,
while for those who rejected him he would become a stone of
stumbling and a rock of offense (a gin and a snare). These would
stumble and fall because of him, taking offense at his doctrines,
and eventually be condemned, broken, and snared. (See Isaiah
8:14–15.) During his mortal ministry the Savior discussed this
prophecy with his disciples, saying that "on whomsoever this stone
shall fall, it shall grind him to powder." (See Matthew 21:33–46.)

The sublime joy of the moment was tempered by the
prophecy of the future. We would understand Simeon's reference to a sword that would pierce Mary's soul as a reference to
the anguish that she would feel as she saw him lifted up on a
Roman cross.

The Witness of Anna
(Luke 2:36–38)

And there was one Anna, a prophetess, the daughter of
Phanuel, of the tribe of Aser: she was of a great age, and
had lived with an husband seven years from her virginity;
     And she was a widow of about fourscore and four years,
which departed not from the temple, but served God with
fastings and prayers night and day.
     And she coming in that instant gave thanks likewise
unto the Lord, and spake of him to all them that looked for
redemption in Jerusalem.

Even as Simeon held the Christ child in his arms a second witness of his divine sonship appeared—the prophetess Anna. This marvelous woman of devotion and spiritual energy would carry her testimony to all the faithful in the Holy City. We cannot be certain from the text whether she was eighty-four years of age or had been a widow for that length of time. It is evident, however, that the temple and the promises given by God to those of the house of Israel were the focal point of her life. She was known by all who frequented the temple regularly, and her testimony would be readily heard.

The Holy Family Returns to Nazareth
(Luke 2:39)

And when they had performed all things according to the law of the Lord, they returned into Galilee, to their own city Nazareth.

Having complied with the requirements of the law in the temple, apparently Joseph and Mary returned to Nazareth. That they did not remain there permanently is evidenced by the fact that the wise men, who would not appear on the scene for at least a year or two, found them in Bethlehem.

An Expanding Circle of Witnesses

"One by one—one of a city and two of a family, as it were—the circle of living witnesses of the Lord's Christ is enlarging. Others besides those involved in the birth of Jesus and of his forerunner are receiving the divine witness and being called to share the burdens always imposed upon those who know truth by the power of the Holy Spirit. Simeon and Anna are now added to the list of true believers. Had they, forty days before in those same temple courts, heard the excited words of the shepherds who saw the angel and heard the heavenly choir? Had they, 'waiting for the consolation of Israel,' hoped to see him in the flesh, perhaps even when his 'parents' came to redeem him from the priests and to purify his mother as the law required?" (*The Mortal Messiah*, 1:354.)

Luke tells us of but two who held and blessed the Christ child in the temple. Surely there were others—if not within the temple courts, in other places—chosen people like Nathanael, of whom the Savior said, "Behold an Israelite indeed, in whom is no guile!" (John 1:47). These would be people ignored by the sacerdotal classes, simple and faithful people who were outside the pale of political rivalry and dispute, people ignorant of the subtleties of Rabbinic argument, people whose personal prayers had reflected those of Zacharias in their pleadings for the birth of their Messiah.

Of Anna, Edersheim observes, "Deepest in her soul was longing waiting for the 'redemption' promised, and now surely nigh. To her widowed heart the great hope of Israel appeared not so much, as to Simeon, in the light of 'consolation,' as rather in that of 'redemption.' The seemingly hopeless exile of her own tribe, the political state of Judaea, the condition—social, moral, and religious—of her own Jerusalem: all kindled in her, as in those who were like-minded, deep, earnest longing for the time of promised 'redemption.' No place so suited to such an one as the Temple, with its services—the only thing free, pure, un-defiled, and pointing forward and upward; no occupation so be-fitting as 'fasting and prayer.' And, blessed be God, there were others, perhaps many such, in Jerusalem. Though Rabbinic tradi-tion ignored them, they were the salt which preserved the mass from festering corruption. To her as the representative, the ex-ample, friend, and adviser of such, was it granted as prophetess to recognize Him, Whose Advent had been the burden of Simeon's praise. And, day by day, to those who looked for re-demption in Jerusalem, would she speak of Him Whom her eyes had seen, though it must be in whispers and with bated breath. For they were in the city of Herod, and the stronghold of Phari-saism." (*The Life and Times of Jesus the Messiah*, p. 140.)

The Importance of Ritual Ceremonies

It is the Gentile Luke who preserves for us the knowledge that Christ was circumcised and named on the eighth day after his birth according to the custom of the Jews. And it is Luke who in like manner preserves for us the knowledge that on the forty-first day after his birth, Mary, his mother, with Joseph, his earthly guardian, went to the temple to present the child to the Lord, make payment of the redemption tax, and comply with the ritual of purification required of Mary. In so doing he errs somewhat in detail over the Jewish law, a circumstance that only adds to the credibility of his story. This is not a story concocted after the fact to give support to a nativity tradition and thus one written by someone knowledgeable in the detail of the law. It is one written in the naiveté of a Gentile who in all likelihood had no real understanding of the importance of Christ's complying with these rituals, their symbolic importance, or the manner in which they testify of his divine sonship.

In circumcision Christ complied with the covenant made with Father Abraham, becoming a child of the law, thus showing that he had not come to destroy Moses and his law but to fulfill them. As an infant in arms he was presented to his divine Father in the temple and there redeemed from the priestly duty so that he might fulfill his destiny as God's Great High Priest. In the purification of his mother we find evidence that all prohibitions of the law were complied with in his birth. In these things we also find him who is destined to be the Messenger of the Covenant assuming all the obligations of that covenant as well as its blessings. All its symbolism was centered in him, and it was for him to honor it most perfectly. These humble yet sacred events sustain his claim to divine sonship.

CHAPTER SEVEN

Wise Men from the East

"There came wise men from the east"

One can be a competent witness of the birth of Christ only on the basis of personal revelation. Such a testimony received in any other way is simply "not of God" (D&C 50:18). Only by the spirit of revelation could the "wise men from the east" have known of a certainty that it was the Son of God to whom they paid homage and gave precious gifts. As with all other witnesses they too must have been just and holy men who had been ordained to the office and call that was theirs in the councils of heaven long before the creation of the earth.

It is not of worshippers of Zoroaster or some sort of priestly-scholars from an ancient mystical order that we speak. It is of prophets of God! Men who held the Melchizedek Priesthood, knew the spirit of revelation, had studied holy writ, conversed with angels, dreamed dreams, and prophesied as did their counterparts among the Nephites. "They knew the King of the Jews had been born, and they knew that a new star was destined to arise and had arisen in connection with that birth. The probability is they were themselves

Herod the King

Jews who lived, as millions of Jews then did, in one of the nations to the East. It was the Jews, not the Gentiles, who were acquainted with the scriptures and who were waiting with anxious expectation for the coming of a King. And that King was to come to them first; he was to deliver his message to them before it went to the Gentile world, and his first witnesses were to come from his own kinsmen, from the house of Israel, not from the Gentile nations, not from the nations composed of those who knew not God and who cared nothing for the spirit of prophecy and revelation found among the Lord's people." (*The Mortal Messiah*, 1:358.)

These special witnesses of the birth of Christ did not come to satisfy their own longings, as did Simeon; they came as representatives of their nations—parts of scattered Israel—to whom they would return to bear their testimony and share the assurance that the long-sought Messiah had now been born. In some future day when the fulness of scriptural records are gathered we anticipate obtaining the testimony they bore to those of the nations from which they came. (See 2 Nephi 29:13–14.)

The Coming of the Wise Men
(Matthew 2:1)

> *Now when Jesus was born in Bethlehem of Judaea in the days of Herod the king, behold, there came wise men from the east to Jerusalem,*

We know not from whence the wise men came. We are told no more than that they came from the east, meaning east of the River Jordan. Reaching out from Jerusalem, this would include the Syro-Arabian desert, Mesopotamia (Babylonia), and Persia. But where the scripures are silent, apocryphal writers become most eloquent. Traditions include the idea that the wise men, or magi, as they are called, "were masters of some astrological cult that could divine great happenings from the stars. They are even named, identified, and described; their ages are given, and the color of their skin; and one can, or could in times past, at least, even view their skulls, crowned with jewels, in a cathedral in Cologne." (*The Mortal Messiah* 1:357.)

Indeed, it might be observed that it is the simplicity of Matthew's account that gives it credibility.

Signs in the Heavens
(Matthew 2:2)

Saying, Where is [the child, JST] he that is born [the Messiah, JST] King of the Jews? for we have seen his star in the east, and are come to worship him.

Our text does not say that the wise men were following a star but rather that they had "seen" the star in the east. How they determined that the star they saw announced the birth of the Messiah we are not told. They, like the Nephites, must have been given the promise of signs in the heavens that would announce Christ's birth. In Helaman 14 we find that prophecy as given by Samuel the Lamanite to the Nephites:

And behold, he said unto them: Behold, I give unto you a sign; for five years more cometh, and behold, then cometh the Son of God to redeem all those who shall believe on his name.

And behold, this will I give unto you for a sign at the time of his coming; for behold, there shall be great lights in heaven, insomuch that in the night before he cometh there shall be no darkness, insomuch that it shall appear unto man as if it was day.

Therefore, there shall be one day and a night and a day, as if it were one day and there were no night; and this shall be unto you for a sign; for ye shall know of the rising of the sun and also of its setting; therefore they shall know of a surety that there shall be two days and a night; nevertheless the night shall not be darkened; and it shall be the night before he is born.

> *And behold, there shall a new star arise, such an one as ye never have beheld; and this also shall be a sign unto you.*
>
> *And behold this is not all, there shall be many signs and wonders in heaven.*
>
> *And it shall come to pass that ye shall all be amazed, and wonder, insomuch that ye shall fall to the earth.*
>
> *And it shall come to pass that whosoever shall believe on the Son of God, the same shall have everlasting life.*

The testimony of the Book of Mormon concerning signs in the heavens attending the birth of Christ becomes particularly important in view of the barrage of criticism leveled at Matthew's account of the star that the wise men are said to have followed. A star that rises in the east, travels at a pace appropriate for its followers, brings them to Jerusalem where it shines over the Holy City, then disappears only to reappear for the wise men but not for others, heads south for five miles to Bethlehem, and then stops over the abode of the Christ child—this is at least a phenomenon unparalleled in astronomical history.

Oceans of ink have been spilt in both debunking and defending the story. Of it we say this with certainty: The stars of heaven were called upon to attest to the birth of Christ, as they will be called upon to announce his second coming. In doing so they need not be bound by those laws normal to their existence. Indeed, we would expect otherwise. As to whether parts of Matthew's narrative represent scriptural hyperbole or are intended to be understood literally, this is left to the reader to determine. It is, nevertheless, difficult to understand how the impression made by such distinguished visitors to a small village with their remarkable gifts would have been of such a nature that Herod's intelligence system could not discover which home they visited and which child they worshipped.

In listing signs that would attend the birth of Christ, Samuel the Lamanite prophesied: "There shall a new star arise, such an one as ye never have beheld" (Helaman 14:5). The star of which he spoke was seen by the whole Nephite nation at the time of Christ's birth. No comparable prophecy exists in the Bible. The nearest allusion is found in the prophecy of Balaam who, speaking of the Messiah, said: "There shall come a Star out of Jacob, and a Sceptre shall rise out of Israel" (Numbers 24:17). Though this prophecy is frequently associated with the story of the wise men it is not without significance that Matthew, who constantly provides us with proof-texts—some of which are rather forced—makes no reference to it.

Herod Seeks to Find the Christ Child
(Matthew 2:3–8)

When Herod the king had heard [of the child, JST] , he was troubled, and all Jerusalem with him.

And when he had gathered all the chief priests and scribes of the people together, he demanded [saying, JST] of them where [is the place that is written of by the prophets, in which] Christ should be born. [For he greatly feared, yet he believed not the prophets.]

And they said unto him, [It is written by the prophets, that he should be born] In Bethlehem of Judaea: for thus [have they said], it is written by the prophet,

[The word of the Lord came unto us, saying], And thou Bethlehem, [which lieth, JST] in the land of Juda, [Judea, in thee shall be born a prince, which] art not the least among the princes of Juda [Judea, JST]: for out of thee shall come a Governor [the Messiah, who], that shall rule [save, JST] my people Israel.

Then Herod, when he had privily called the wise men, enquired of them diligently what time the star appeared.

And he sent them to Bethlehem, and said, Go and search diligently for the young child; and when ye have found him, bring me word again, that I may come and worship him also.

There is nothing in the story of the birth of Christ that suggests it was to be a secret; rather we find it witnessed throughout

both the heavens and the earth. Wise men from the east announced it to King Herod, who would not have given audience
to lowly shepherds or the likes of Simeon and Anna. Through
Herod the testimony of the wise men was made known to "all
the chief priests and scribes" and "all Jerusalem." The fact that
more than one chief priest is mentioned suggests that the office
had become a lucrative one and thus frequently changed hands
(see *Vincent's Word Studies*, p. 20).

Our friend Farrar writes:

> *Herod the Great, who, after a life of splendid misery*
> *and criminal success, had now sunk into the jealous de-*
> *crepitude of his savage old age, was residing in his new*
> *palace on Zion, when, half maddened as he was already by*
> *the crimes of his past career, he was thrown into a fresh*
> *paroxysm of alarm and anxiety by the visit of some Eastern*
> *Magi, bearing the strange intelligence that they had seen in*
> *the East the star of a new-born king of the Jews, and had*
> *come to worship him. Herod, a mere Idumaean usurper, a*
> *more than suspected apostate, the detested tyrant over an*
> *unwilling people, the sacrilegious plunderer of the tomb of*
> *David—Herod, a descendant of the despised Ishmael and*
> *the hated Esau, heard the tidings with a terror and indig-*
> *nation which it was hard to dissimulate. The grandson of*
> *one who, as was believed, had been a mere servitor in a*
> *temple at Ascalon, and who in his youth had been carried*
> *off by Edomite brigands, he well knew how worthless were*
> *his pretensions to an historic throne which he held solely by*
> *successful adventure. But his craft equalled his cruelty, and*
> *finding that all Jerusalem shared his suspense, he sum-*
> *moned to his palace the leading priests and theologians of*
> *the Jews—perhaps the relics of that Sanhedrin which he had*
> *long reduced to a despicable shadow—to inquire of them*
> *where the Messiah was to be born. He received the ready*
> *and confident answer that Bethlehem was the town indi-*
> *cated for that honour by the prophecy of Micah. Concealing,*

therefore, his desperate intention, he dispatched the wise men to Bethlehem, bidding them to let him know as soon as they had found the child, that he too might come and do him reverence." (The Life of Christ, *pp. 48–49.*)

In his rage over family rivalries and jealousies Herod had put to death many people. He had made will after will and was now in a fatal illness and fury over the testimony of his visitors from the east. The people of Jerusalem, knowing only too well of his rage, could hardly remain ignorant of what was taking place or the danger it threatened.

"His whole career was red with the blood of murder. He had massacred priests and nobles; he had decimated the Sanhedrin; he had caused the High Priest, his brother-in-law, the young and noble Aristobulus, to be drowned in pretended sport before his eyes; he had ordered the strangulation of his favorite wife, the beautiful Asmonaean princess Mariamne, though she seems to have been the only human being whom he passionately loved. His sons Alexander, Aristobulus, and Antipater—his uncle Joseph—Antigonus and Alexander, the uncle and father of his wife—his mother-in-law Alexandra—his kinsman Cortobanus— his friends Dositheus and Gadias, were but a few of the multitudes who fell victims to his sanguinary, suspicious, and guilty terrors. His brother Pheroras and his son Archelaus barely and narrowly escaped execution by his orders. Neither the blooming youth of the prince Aristobulus nor the white hairs of the king Hyrcanus had protected them from his fawning and treacherous fury. Deaths by strangulation, deaths by burning, deaths by being cleft asunder, deaths by secret assassination, confessions forced by unutterable torture, acts of insolent and inhuman lust, mark the annals of a reign which was so cruel that, in the energetic language of the Jewish ambassadors to the Emperor Augustus, 'the survivors during his lifetime were even more miserable than the sufferers.' . . . Every dark and brutal instinct of his character seemed to acquire fresh intensity as his life drew towards its close. Haunted by the spectres of his murdered wife and murdered sons, agitated by the conflicting furies of remorse and blood, the pitiless monster, as Josephus calls him, was seized in his last days by a black and bitter ferocity, which broke out against all with whom he came in contact." (*The Life of Christ,* pp. 61–62.)

The Light of the Star Returns
(Matthew 2:9–10)

When they had heard the king, they departed; and, lo, the star, which they saw in the east, went before them, till it came and stood over where the young child was.

When they saw the star, they rejoiced with exceeding great joy.

It appears that after the wise men left Herod the star they "saw in the east, went before them" once again. Apparently they alone could see and follow the light that led from Jerusalem to the house in Bethlehem in which the Christ child was to be found. Were this not the case, Herod and those who did his bidding would have had no need of them. In the providence of the Lord it was necessary that the testimony of the birth of Israel's rightful king be borne to the wicked usurper Herod.

The Wise Men Worship Christ
(Matthew 2:11)

And when they were come into the house, they saw the young child with Mary his mother, and fell down, and worshipped him: and when they had opened their treasures, they presented unto him gifts; gold, and frankincense, and myrrh.

Some measurable time had now elapsed from the day of Christ's birth. The visit of the wise men was not made to the stable where Christ was born. It was a "house" to which they came and a "young child" that they worshipped, not a newborn infant. Herod's edict to have all male children two years and younger slain represented the approximate age of the child.

That the wise men would fall down to worship the young child suggests that the homage they felt for him was beyond that of pagan star worshippers.

The gifts brought to the Christ child seem to carry with them a special symbolic significance. By tradition gold is thought to be the gift of royalty, symbolizing their recognition of Christ as their king and of his being of royal descent; myrrh is the symbol of humanity which would be represented in his death; and incense the acknowledgment of his divinity in his rising again.

The Wise Men Warned of God
(Matthew 2:12)

And being warned of God in a dream that they should not return to Herod, they departed into their own country another way.

That the wise men dreamed dreams and received revelation from God is but another evidence that they were prophets called and ordained in the proper manner. The Lord's house has ever been a house of order.

Joseph Warned in a Dream
(Matthew 2:13–15)

And when they were departed, behold, the angel of the Lord appeareth to Joseph in a dream, saying, Arise, and take the young child and his mother, and flee into Egypt, and be thou there until I bring thee word: for Herod will seek the young child to destroy him.

When he arose, he took the young child and his mother by night, and departed into Egypt:

And was there until the death of Herod: that it might

be fulfilled which was spoken of the Lord by the prophet, saying, Out of Egypt have I called my son.

Joseph did not hesitate. The Holy Family left immediately by
the dark of night. They would have sought to travel unnoticed
down through the hill country of Judea passing through Hebron
and Beersheba, which would be the beginning of barren waste-
land. Here they would turn right toward the Mediterranean and
Gaza, where they could join a caravan of travelers going to
Egypt. They could not travel safely alone. The journey of more
than two hundred miles would have taken ten or twelve days.

*It is left to apocryphal legends, immortalized by the
genius of Italian art, to tell us how, on the way, the dragons
came and bowed to Him, the lions and leopards adored
Him, the roses of Jericho blossomed wherever His footsteps
trod, the palm-trees at His command bent down to give
them dates, the robbers were overawed by His majesty, and
the journey was miraculously shortened. They tell us further
how, at His entrance into the country, all the idols of the
land of Egypt fell from their pedestals with a sudden crash,
and lay shattered and broken upon their faces, and how
many wonderful cures of leprosy and demoniac possession
were wrought by His word. All this wealth and prodigality
of superfluous, aimless, and unmeaning miracle . . . fur-
nishes a strong contrast to the truthful simplicity of the
Gospel narrative.* (The Life of Christ, p. 58.)

Of significance in this story is that the revelation for the
safety of the family comes to Joseph, not Mary. Joseph is the
head, and it is for him to provide and protect. Mary does not
question or cause delay. She looks to Joseph and follows.

At the direction of the angel Joseph takes Mary and the child
into Egypt for a time and season yet to be revealed. This that "it
might be fulfilled which was spoken of the Lord by the prophet,
saying, Out of Egypt have I called my son"—so that whenever

Israel remembers how God had delivered them with a mighty hand from the bondage of Egypt, they will think also that the Son of God was called out of Egypt to deliver them from the bondage of sin.

Significantly, it was one bearing the name Joseph who provided safety for the house of Israel in Egypt anciently when famine swept the land. From Joseph they received the bread of life and were saved. Thence the Lord's chosen people came out of Egypt into their land of promise, where they were to build his temple and walk in his paths. So it was that his Beloved and Chosen would now come out of that same land to restore his gospel and invite the chosen seed to walk in the appointed course.

As the children of Israel had been delivered from their Egyptian bondage by great miracles, so they were now to receive an even greater deliverance, one that would free them from every bondage of the flesh and return them to a greater and an eternal land of promise at the hands of their promised Messiah. Well might it be said that this very event in the history of the Jews pointed to Christ's coming and ministry among them.

So it would be again in the last days when one bearing the name Joseph would bring the knowledge of the true Messiah back to the chosen people of the Lord. That the type might be perfect, he too would fill his calling with angelic direction.

Herod Slaughters the Children
(Matthew 2:16–18)

> *Then Herod, when he saw that he was mocked of the wise men, was exceeding wroth, and sent forth, and slew all the children that were in Bethlehem, and in all the coasts thereof, from two years old and under, according to the time which he had diligently enquired of the wise men.*
>
> *Then was fulfilled that which was spoken by Jeremy the prophet, saying,*
>
> *In Rama was there a voice heard, lamentation, and weeping, and great mourning, Rachel weeping for her children, and would not be comforted, because they are not.*

That it was male children only, rather than "all the children" as the King James Version renders it, is generally accepted. The reference to "the coasts thereof" is an archaic use of the word that simply means "regions." The number of children killed is generally thought to be twenty or less (see Edersheim, *The Life and Times of Jesus the Messiah*, p. 149). Numbers, however, had nothing to do with Herod's wrath; to protect his office he would kill all that he had to kill, regardless of their innocence and even though he was on his deathbed. Herod's edict would have been fixed from the time the wise men first saw the star. He died in 4 B.C., which suggests that Christ was born in 6 B.C., though it could be noted that a child is two years of age until his third birthday.

Jacob's wife Rachel died and was buried on the way from Bethel to Ephrath. This took place about five miles north of Jerusalem. Later Christian tradition, however, identified the place of her burial as being on the road between Jerusalem and Bethlehem, which is to the south of the Holy City. In his writing Jeremiah speaks of Rachel, the ancestress of Benjamin and Ephraim, rising from her place of rest to lament the loss of her children when the northern tribes were taken into exile. In this text, Matthew draws upon the imagery of her sorrow and applies it to Herod's slaughter of the infants in and around Bethlehem.

That He Might Be Called a Nazarene
(Matthew 2:19–23)

> *But when Herod was dead, behold, an angel of the Lord appeareth in a dream to Joseph in Egypt,*
>
> *Saying, Arise, and take the young child and his mother, and go into the land of Israel: for they are dead which sought the young child's life.*
>
> *And he arose, and took the young child and his mother, and came into the land of Israel.*
>
> *But when he heard that Archelaus did reign in Judaea in the room of his father Herod, he was afraid to go thither: notwithstanding, being warned of God in a dream, he turned aside into the parts of Galilee:*

> *And he came and dwelt in a city called Nazareth: that*
> *it might be fulfilled which was spoken by the prophets, He*
> *shall be called a Nazarene.*

Herod was now dead. This Joseph learned from the angel of the Lord, who told the Holy Family to return to Palestine. From passing travelers the message of Herod's death was confirmed and Joseph learned that Archelaus, Herod's oldest surviving son, ruled in his stead. History attests that Archelaus possessed the same evil disposition as his father.

It was required that the Holy Family proceed in faith, obtaining understanding and direction line upon line. When the angel came to tell them that they were to leave Egypt, the direction was only that they were now to return to the land of Israel. It was absolutely essential that they go to Nazareth, but they were not so told. Their inclination was to go to Judaea, yet one senses that they had uneasy feelings about it when they learned that Archelaus ruled. It would seem only natural that they would make it a matter of prayer, in response to which a dream was given that directed them to Galilee.

Prophecy, now lost to us but known to Matthew, held that the Messiah would be called a Nazarene. The name was one of contempt. In Hebrew it means "sprout," or "shoot." Speaking prophetically Isaiah had said: "And there shall come forth a rod out of the stem of Jesse, and a Branch shall grow out of his roots" (Isaiah 11:1). The text could also be rendered, "A shoot will come up from the stump of Jesse, from his roots a twig will bear fruit." "As David sprang from the humble family of Jesse, so the Messiah, the second David, shall arise out of great humiliation. The fact that Jesus grew up at Nazareth was sufficient reason for his being despised. He was not a lofty branch on the summit of a stately tree; not a recognized and honored son of the royal house of David, now fallen, but an insignificant *sprout* from the roots of Jesse; a Nazarene, of an upstart sprout-town." (Marvin R. Vincent, *Word Studies in the New Testament,* McLean, Va.: Macdonald Publishing Company, n.d., p. 22.)

The Testimony of Heaven and Hell

As signs in the heavens attest to the faithful of the birth of their Messiah so the wrath of hell as manifest through one of its chief servants, King Herod, assures us of the rage of the kingdom of darkness. So it ever is. The peaceable things of the kingdom find opposition in that spirit that knows no peace, and the birth of the Prince of Peace stands opposed by him who rules in darkness.

In the coming of the wise men the nation of the Jews was reminded that others also pay homage to their king and seek salvation in his name.

CHAPTER EIGHT

Twelve Witnesses
of Christ's Birth

*The holy family fled
by night into Egypt*

T his thing was not done in a corner," Paul said of Christ's ministry and the restoration of the gospel in the meridian of time (Acts 26:26). In like manner we discover that the birth of Christ was heralded among the faithful of every nation, kindred, tongue, and people. Indeed, the witnesses of the Savior's birth were many and various. Samuel prophesied to those in the Americas of the signs of his coming (see Helaman 14:3–6), and Alma wrote that the story of Christ's birth would be heralded by angels to men who were "just and holy" (Alma 13:26). In the nation of Christ's birth, the testimony of his coming went forth in ever-widening circles—especially among those blameless in keeping the commandments of the Lord and filled with the Holy Ghost. Together Matthew and Luke provide us with twelve witnesses to the nativity. Although their individual testimonies themselves are remarkable, their collective testimony constitutes a powerful witness of Christ's birth. As their stories unfold, every appropriate element appears in its proper place, which is all the more remarkable since the two writers each tell different parts of the story.

The nativity story begins with an angelic announcement within the holy place of the temple to a priest whose prayer on behalf of his nation has just pleaded for that very event. With equal propriety, it ends with the announcement of Herod's evil designs upon the Christ child's life. Within the story we see the heavens opened to priest and layman, to man and woman, to old and young, to the mighty and to the humble. We see each called to be a witness in this matchless drama of a God coming to earth through birth to a mortal woman in the humblest of circumstances to accomplish the most exalted of purposes. It is a matchless story.

Gabriel

Our first New Testament witness of the birth of Christ was a messenger from the presence of God: Gabriel. Appropriately, this messenger made his initial appearance in the temple to a faithful priest of the Aaronic order, Zacharias, who was performing a ritual function on behalf of his nation—burning incense on the altar within the Holy Place.

In performing this duty Zacharias represented the combined faith of Israel. His prayer was their prayer for an everlasting deliverance from all their enemies at the hands of their promised Messiah. The ascending smoke of incense symbolized the ascension of that united prayer. As Zacharias prayed, his fellow priests and all within the walls of the temple united their amens with his appeal.

In response to Israel's prayer, an "angel of the Lord" appeared before Zacharias, standing on the right side of the altar of incense and identifying himself as Gabriel, one who stood "in the presence of God" (Luke 1:11, 19). By modern revelation we know that Gabriel was known on earth as Noah, that he "stands next in authority to Adam in the Priesthood" (*Teachings*, 157), and that he holds the keys of the "restoration of all things" (D&C 27:6–7).

The keys held by Gabriel made him an Elias to prepare the way before the Lord. How perfectly appropriate, then, for him to announce the birth of the earthly Elias, John the Baptist, who would prepare the way for the Messiah.

Zacharias

Who was this Zacharias to whom Gabriel appeared? He was one of the "just and holy," as was his wife, Elisabeth (see Luke 1:6). Zacharias was a descendant of Abia, whose name meant, "remembered of Jehovah." Elisabeth, like Zacharias, was a descendant of priests (see Luke 1:5), and her name meant "consecrated to God."

Thus this noble couple were, in the nativity story, to be remembered of Jehovah. Promised a child destined to be the earthly forerunner of the Messiah, Zacharias received the sign from Gabriel that he would remain "not able to speak, until the day that these things shall be performed," because he did not believe the Lord's prophetic promise (see Luke 1:20).

He remained mute until "Elisabeth's full time came that she should be delivered." It was then that Zacharias' "mouth was opened" and he bore witness of the divine mission of his newborn son, testifying that he would "go before the face of the Lord to prepare his ways." News of these miraculous occurrences "were noised abroad throughout Judea" (vv. 57, 64, 65, 76).

Elisabeth

We read of John that he was "filled with the Holy Ghost, even from his mother's womb" (Luke 1:15). Indeed, when Mary visited Elisabeth, "Elisabeth heard the salutation of Mary [and] the babe leaped in her womb; and Elisabeth was filled with the Holy Ghost" (Luke 1:41).

As a pure vessel who recognized the special nature of her own son, Elisabeth also testified and bore witness of the divinity of Mary's son, crying: "Blessed art thou among women, and blessed is the fruit of thy womb. And whence is this to me, that the mother of my Lord should come to me?" (Luke 1:42–43.)

Elisabeth concluded her witness by prophesying that "there shall be a performance of those things which were told her from the Lord" (Luke 1:45). She added her testimony to those who came before and those who followed in declaring the divine birth.

John the Baptist

As Christ was, by birth, the rightful heir to David's kingdom, so John was born the rightful heir of the office of Elias. He appropriately began his ministry, to "go before the face of the Lord to prepare his ways," by leaping for joy while yet within his mother's womb (Luke 1:41, 76; see also v. 15).

What a marvelous event it must have been: John leaping for joy; Elisabeth greeting her cousin Mary in the spirit of prophecy; and Mary responding by that same spirit. Again we note how wondrously the witnesses and testimonies fit together: the testimonies of the two women—the aged Elisabeth and the youthful Mary—each bearing a child conceived under miraculous circumstances. They, and even the unborn John, all rejoiced in the great event about to take place.

Mary

There could be no more perfect mortal witness of Christ's divine sonship than his mother, Mary. From Gabriel she received the promise that she would conceive in her womb "the Son of the Highest" (Luke 1:32). Following that marvelous event, she testified, saying, "He that is mighty hath done to me great things; and holy is his name" (Luke 1:49).

Nephi gave us a perfect scriptural account of this most sacred event. "And it came to pass," he wrote, "that I beheld that she was carried away in the Spirit; and after she had been carried away in the Spirit for the space of a time the angel spake unto me, saying: Look! And I looked and beheld the virgin again, bearing a child in her arms. And the angel said unto me: Behold the Lamb of God, yea even the Son of the Eternal Father!" (1 Nephi 11:19–21.)

Truly Mary was, as Gabriel told her, "highly favored" and "blessed . . . among women" to have witnessed these miracles and to have given birth to the Savior (Luke 1:28).

Joseph

We have no scriptural record of any words spoken by Joseph, yet his righteousness and his reactions to Mary's condition bear testimony to his belief in Christ's divine sonship. We know that he dreamed dreams and entertained angels. Further we know that he was faithful in keeping the law of Moses and that he faithfully heeded each divine direction that was given him.

He displayed unquestioning obedience in taking Mary, already carrying a child, as his wife after "the angel of the Lord appeared unto him in a dream, saying, Joseph, thou son of David, fear not to take unto thee Mary thy wife: for that which is conceived in her is of the Holy Ghost" (Matthew 1:20). He also "knew her not till she had brought forth her firstborn son"; named the son Jesus; fled by night with Mary and the child to Egypt; remained in Egypt until directed to return; and returned to Galilee rather than to Judea (Matthew 1:25; see also vv. 19–21; 2:13–23).

Each of these actions witnessed anew Joseph's conviction regarding the child, the hope of Israel, the Son of God.

The Shepherds

On the eve of Christ's birth in the stable at Bethlehem, shepherds watched over their flocks in fields not far distant. These were not ordinary shepherds, for it had been prophesied among the Nephites that angels would declare the glad tidings of the Messiah's birth to "just and holy men" (Alma 13:26).

The special witnesses borne by these shepherds were to be told to family, friends, and neighbors. They were to be told in the courts of the temple, and from there to be told among all nations of the earth. Luke tells us that after the shepherds had seen the "babe lying in a manger, . . . they made known abroad the saying which was told them concerning this child" (Luke 2:16–17). Such was the declaration of the angel who stood before them that holy night, that these "good tidings" should "be to all people" (Luke 2:10).

The Heavenly Choir

Following the angel's announcement to the shepherds, "suddenly there was . . . a multitude of the heavenly host praising God" (Luke 2:13). The heavenly choir then sang to the humble shepherds of Judea "Glory to God in the highest, and on earth peace, good will toward men" (Luke 2:14), heralding with music the Savior's birth among the scattered remnants of Israel.

Simeon

Our attention now turns to Jerusalem. There an aged man, described by Luke as "just and devout," who had received the promise of the Lord that he would not die until he had seen the Savior, was moved upon by the Holy Ghost to go to the temple. There he held the Christ child.

When the parents and the child entered the temple—Mary to comply with the required ritual cleansing and Joseph to pay the tax necessary to redeem the firstborn from priestly service—Simeon took the child in his arms. "Lord, now lettest thou thy servant depart in peace, according to thy word," he declared. "For mine eyes have seen thy salvation, which thou hast prepared before the face of all people; A light to lighten the Gentiles and the glory of thy people Israel." (Luke 2:29–32.)

Simeon's declaration reached far beyond the understanding and hope of those of his nation, for he saw the universal nature of Christ's ministry. He bore witness that Jesus was the Savior to Jew and Gentile alike.

Anna

The marvelous testimony of Simeon was not to stand alone. Joining his special witness, which has echoed forth from the temple down through the generations, was Anna, the aged widow whose name means "full of grace." A devout and saintly woman who worshipped for many years in the temple with fasting and prayer both day and night, she was well known to those of the Holy City who faithfully sought the coming of the Messiah. She approached the holy family and thereafter bore testimony of the Messiah to those in Jerusalem who "looked for redemption" (Luke 2:38).

The Wise Men from the East

Matthew alone makes reference to the coming of the wise men some time after the Savior's birth, writing, "There came wise men from the east to Jerusalem" (Matthew 2:1). We know that the wise men were ignorant of the political situation at the time, for they sought Christ's whereabouts from Herod: "Where is he that is born King of the Jews? for we have seen his star in the east, and are come to worship him" (Matthew 2:2). No one who knew Herod would have endangered the life of Christ by asking such a question of him.

We also know that they were visionary men, for they were later "warned of God in a dream that they should not return to Herod" and consequently "departed into their own country another way" (Matthew 2:12).

Herod

Our concluding witness is a most unlikely and reluctant one—Israel's king, Herod the Great. Herod had made an alliance with the powers of the world: his friends were Augustus, Rome, and expediency. He had massacred priests and nobles. He had decimated the Sanhedrin. He had caused the high priest, his brother-in-law, to be drowned in pretended sport before his eyes. And he had ordered the strangulation of his favorite wife, Mariamne, though she seems to have been the only person he ever loved. Anyone who fell victim to his suspicions was murdered, including three of his sons and numerous relatives.

It was to this man, who personified the world's wickedness, that the wise men from the east bore their testimony that Israel's rightful king and ruler had been born. Such a testimony would not have been heeded had it come from Simeon, Anna, or simple shepherds. But Herod gave the testimony credence, coming as it did from these Eastern visitors, whose credentials, whatever they were, established them as men of great wisdom.

The kingdom of God will never go unopposed in the days of the earth's mortality, the period of Satan's power. Evidence of the anger and wrath of hell at the birth of God's Son makes the nativity story complete. The tidings of great joy brought no joy to the prince of darkness or his servants. Herod, as Satan's servant, responded to the testimony of the wise men with murderous wrath and sought to destroy the Christ child. Thus the decree went forth that "all the children that were in Bethlehem, and in all the coasts thereof, from two years old and under," according to the time when Herod had inquired of the wise men, were to be slain (see Matthew 2:16).

Conclusion

The nativity story, as it is preserved for us in the New Testament, mentions twelve witnesses of the birth of the Savior and illustrates the pattern by which the knowledge of God is to be restored and to go forth once again among all the nations of the earth.

How will it go forth? By special witnesses—witnesses called and prepared in the councils of heaven. Who will they be? The old and the young, women and men, the learned and the unlearned—those who walk "in all the commandments and ordinances of the Lord blameless," those who dream dreams, entertain angels, and are filled with the Holy Ghost (Luke 1:6). So it ever has been, and so it must ever be.

Epilogue: "Who Shall Declare His Generation?"

"Mary kept all these things, and pondered them in her heart"

The Gospel of Matthew begins: "The book of the generation of Jesus Christ, the son of David." In so writing, Matthew, who is addressing himself to the Jews and frequently draws upon scriptural texts with which they are familiar, is responding to the language of Isaiah in what is generally agreed to be the greatest Messianic prophecy in the Old Testament. In the midst of his description of the Messiah, Isaiah asked, "Who shall declare his generation?" (Isaiah 53:8.) That is, whose testimony can we trust in telling the story of Christ's progenitors. That he be of the right lineage was understood by all to be absolutely necessary. The promise of scripture was that the Messiah would be a descendant of David and thus have rightful claim on his progenitor's throne. Of greater moment still was his right to claim sonship from God that he might also sit upon a heavenly throne. These are the issues to which Matthew responds in order to prove that Jesus of Nazareth was the rightful heir of the Messianic office. Similarly, if we are to prove ourselves the rightful heirs of his gospel and bearers of the authority to speak in his name, we must respond to these same issues and also be competent witnesses of the divine sonship of Jesus of Nazareth.

The Genealogies Given by Matthew and Luke

Matthew provides us with a genealogical line from Abraham to "Joseph the husband of Mary, of whom was born Jesus, who is called Christ" (Matthew 1:1–16). Luke also gives a genealogy for Christ, starting with Joseph, which traces back to Adam. His account, however, does not conform to Matthew's (see Luke 3:23–28). Responding to this difficulty, Elder Bruce R. McConkie comments: "Scholars are unable to unravel or bring into harmony the accounts here involved, and we have not been told by revelation the specifics of our Lord's ancestry. There is no way from a historical standpoint to search out the generation of Christ. One of the Biblical accounts may be the genealogy of Mary, the other of Joseph; one may assay to set forth kingly descent, the other give the lineal ancestry. We do not know. The only point upon which there is surety is the fact that Mary was his mother and God was his Father; other than that, his generation, his genesis, his beginnings are lost in antiquity except for a few obvious facts, as we shall now note.

"'Blessed is he [Noah] through whose seed Messiah shall come,' the Lord said to Enoch. We know in general terms and within a broad framework who some of his ancestors were. Manifestly he is a descendant of Adam, the first man. Indeed, the first Messianic prophecy of which we have record was spoken to Eve, 'the mother of all living' (Genesis 3:20), while she and Adam were yet in Eden's garden. 'I will put enmity between thee and the woman,' the Lord said to Lucifer, 'between thy seed and her seed [the seed of woman or the seed of Mary]; and he shall bruise thy head, and thou shalt bruise his heel.' (Moses 4:21.) Ever since, the seed of Satan, those who follow him, have thwarted and plagued the Lord's work, as far as in them lay, with the ultimate triumph and success in the great warfare of life being reserved for Him as he crushes Satan and his followers under his heel.

"Manifestly our Lord's descent, going downward, is Adam,

Seth, Enos, Cainan, Mahalaleel, Jared, Enoch, Methuselah, Lamech, and Noah. It was to Noah that the Lord said, 'With thee will I establish my covenant, even as I have sworn unto thy father Enoch, that of thy posterity shall come all nations.' (JST, Genesis 8:23.) After Noah we go down through Shem to Abraham, Isaac, Jacob, and Judah. In that tribe we center in David, and then the problem of tracing descent is beyond our ability to solve." (*The Promised Messiah*, Salt Lake City: Deseret Book, 1978, pp. 471–72.)

Matthew's Rendering of Christ's Genealogy (Matthew 1:1–2)

The book of the generation of Jesus Christ, the son of David, the son of Abraham.

Abraham begat Isaac; and Isaac begat Jacob; and Jacob begat Judas and his brethren;

In his lead sentence Matthew affirms that which is universally understood by the Jews, that their Messiah will be the descendant of both Abraham and David (see Galatians 3:16; Psalm 132:11; Isaiah 9:7; Isaiah 11:1–5; Jeremiah 23:5).

The Oxford Dictionary on Historical Principles defines "generation" as the "act or process of generating or begetting." Procreation is used as its synonym. Matthew 1:1 is then cited as an illustration of the point. Having done so, and this would have to rank as an unusual departure from the formality associated with such a work, its authors cannot constrain themselves from an observation, suggesting that the notion that the Father and the Son are of the same essence, as announced in creeds of Christendom, violates both logic and the plain meaning of words. Their entry reads: "Strange G. [generation] this? Father and Son Co-eval [existing simultaneous], two distinct and yet but one Ken." (William Little et al. *The Shorter Oxford English Dictionary on Historical Principles*, Oxford: Clarendon Press, 1936, 1:784.)

The Progenitors of Christ
(Matthew 1:3–7)

And Judas begat Phares and Zara of Thamar; and Phares begat Esrom; and Esrom begat Aram;

And Aram begat Aminadab; and Aminadab begat Naasson; and Naasson begat Salmon;

And Salmon begat Booz of Rachab; and Booz begat Obed of Ruth; and Obed begat Jesse;

And Jesse begat David the king; and David the king begat Solomon of her that had been the wife of Urias;

And Solomon begat Roboam; and Roboam begat Abia; and Abia begat Asa;

Significantly, Matthew departs from the traditional pattern of citing only the father's name in order to introduce four of Jesus' maternal ancestors. (The naming of women was not permitted in Hebrew genealogical tables; see *Clarke's Commentary* 1:383.) All four women named—Thamar, Rachab, Ruth, and Bathsheba (Urias' wife)—could as part of the Old Testament story be regarded as sinners. "Tamar was a seductress and pretended prostitute; Rachab was a prostitute;" Bathsheba an adulteress; and Ruth a non-Israelite who as such worshipped false gods. Notwithstanding their difficulties, each of these women were held in honor (see Raymond E. Brown, *The Birth of the Messiah*, New York: Doubleday, 1993, p. 72). This, it would appear, was Matthew's subtle response to the concern about Mary being with child before her marriage to Joseph.

Christ's Progenitors Continued
(Matthew 1:8–16)

And Asa begat Josaphat; and Josaphat begat Joram; and Joram begat Ozias;

And Ozias begat Joatham; and Joatham begat Achaz; and Achaz begat Ezekias;

And Ezekias begat Manasses; and Manasses begat Amon; and Amon begat Josias;

And Josias begat Jechonias and his brethren, about the time they were carried away to Babylon:

And after they were brought to Babylon, Jechonias begat Salathiel; and Salathiel begat Zorobabel;

And Zorobabel begat Abiud; and Abiud begat Eliakim; and Eliakim begat Azor;

And Azor begat Sadoc; and Sadoc begat Achim; and Achim begat Eliud;

And Eliud begat Eleazar; and Eleazar begat Matthan; and Matthan begat Jacob;

And Jacob begat Joseph the husband of Mary, of whom was born Jesus, who is called Christ.

After having rehearsed the history of who "begat" whom from generation to generation, Matthew deliberately shifts from that pattern to announce the birth of Christ. This is done so that he does not suggest that Joseph is Jesus' biological father.

The word *begat,* as used in the previous verses, need not always mean immediate parentage, but can mean merely direct descent. For instance, the scriptures refer to Abraham, Isaac, and Jacob as our fathers. We are their sons and daughters, though generations separate us from them.

Matthew's Formula of Three Generations of Fourteen (Matthew 1:17)

So all the generations from Abraham to David are fourteen generations; and from David until the carrying away into Babylon are fourteen generations; and from the carrying away into Babylon unto Christ are fourteen generations.

Matthew's division of the genealogy of Christ into three parts having fourteen generations in each is contrived. Things simply don't add up. In the first section, Abraham to David, there are fourteen names but only thirteen generations. In the second section, from David to the Babylonian Exile, there are fourteen generations listed, though this can only be accomplished by omitting four historical generations and six kings. In the third section, from the Babylonian Exile to Jesus, only thirteen generations are listed (see Brown, *The Birth of the Messiah,* pp. 81–82).

"The spans of time covered by the three sections of the genealogy are too great to have contained only fourteen generations each, since some 750 years separated Abraham from David, some 400 years separated David from the Babylonian Exile, and some 600 years separated the Babylonian Exile from Jesus' birth" (Brown, *The Birth of the Messiah,* pp. 74–75).

It seems strange that Matthew would call his readers' attention to the 3 x 14 pattern as something providential when it represents neither good math nor good history. Matthew's overriding purpose is to show that Jesus is the Davidic Messiah. His 3 x 14 pattern seems to be an attempt to relate this in a mystical way to his Jewish readers. In Hebrew orthography a numerical value was given to each letter in the alphabet. Messages were then sought in the numbers of various words. Such a message is found here in the name David. The Hebrew letter *daleth* [d] has a value of four, and *waw* [v] of six. David's name, which was rendered without vowels, consisted of three letters dvd, thus its numerical value would be 4 + 6 + 4 or fourteen. Thus in the name David, Matthew was able to find three generations of fourteen, which he interpreted to point to the Davidic Messiah.

Luke's Rendering of Christ's Genealogy

Matthew and Luke provide genealogies of Christ for very different purposes. As seen, Matthew is at lengths to establish Jesus' claim to the throne of David. Luke, on the other hand, takes a more universal view. He also carefully disassociates Joseph from the fatherhood of Christ (see Luke 3:23). His purpose is to identify the life of Jesus not only with the seed of Abraham but also with all mankind, and thus he lists his ancestors all the way back to Adam, "who was formed of God, and the first man upon the earth" (see JST Luke 3:30–45).

Declaring the Generation of Christ

As we conclude this work we return again to the question asked by Isaiah in his great Messianic prophecy: "Who shall declare his generation?" for it is in answering this question that the true Messiah and his witnesses are to be found. Knowing that God is everlastingly the same, we simply seek that system of declaring Christ that conforms to the scriptural pattern followed in the declaration of his birth. As his birth was announced by angels, we would look for a people who possessed the keys of the ministering of angels. That is, for instance, a people whose testimony of both the birth and the return of the Messiah rested upon the declaration of angels to those of their immediate number. As others in that ancient day received the witness of Christ's birth by revelation or through the Holy Ghost, we would expect the same to be true in our day.

For those of both dispensations the channel of knowledge must be the same. Surely for such a people the heavens cannot be sealed and the canon of scripture cannot be complete. We would also expect, as was the case at the time of Christ, that the special witnesses produced by such experiences would include old and young, male and female, those of high station and those of no social standing.

Also in harmony with the biblical pattern, we would expect this testimony of Christ to come to us from those of the family of Abraham. The promise was given him that both the Messiah and all who ministered in the Savior's name would be his seed (see Abraham 2:9–11). Thus central among their doctrines as they sought to bring people to Christ would be the promises made to the fathers relative to the gathering of Israel, the return of the ten tribes, and the restoration of both remnants of Jacob to their various lands of promise. Nephi described that which would happen in this language:

And after they have been scattered, and the Lord God hath scourged them by other nations for the space of many generations, yea, even down from generation to generation until they shall be persuaded to believe in Christ, the Son of God, and the atonement, which is infinite for all mankind—and when that day shall come that they shall believe in Christ, and worship the Father in his name, with pure hearts and clean hands, and look not forward any more for another Messiah, then, at that time, the day will come that it must needs be expedient that they should believe these things.

And the Lord will set his hand again the second time to restore his people from their lost and fallen state. Wherefore, he will proceed to do a marvelous work and wonder among the children of men. (2 Nephi 25:16–17.)

As was the case with John the Baptist, we would expect to find these latter-day ministers of Christ declaring the doctrine of repentance and baptism by immersion for the remission of sins. In all ages the Lord's people have been a covenant people, a covenant first made in the waters of baptism, and have taken upon them the name of their Master, seeking salvation in his name and in no other.

The nature of the testimony of which we speak can only be borne by the power of the Spirit. As noted, it must come by revelation. This too was part of the declaration of Isaiah, for in that same text in which he asked the question, "Who shall declare his generation," he also asked, "To whom is the arm of the Lord revealed?" (Isaiah 53:1.) The answer was given by Nephi, who said it was those to whom the Lord will reveal "his covenants and his gospel." As Latter-day Saints we possess both. Nephi further explained that to "make bare his arm in the eyes of all nations," according to the prophecy of Isaiah, was to declare the gospel among all nations. (1 Nephi 22:10–11.)

Elder Bruce R. McConkie responds to this question in this manner:

*Now, if we want to know who is going to declare his
generation, the answer is that it is the Latter-day Saints; it
is the elders of Israel; it is the prophets and apostles who
minister among us; and it is all of those among us who have
lived in such a manner that we know by the whisperings of
the Holy Spirit within us that here is eternal verity, that
these things are true. You can be one, as well as I can be
one, who declares the generation of Jesus Christ, who gives
his genealogy, who comes to know in his heart by a power
that is beyond intellectuality, by a power that comes from
revelation and revelation only, that he is the Lord, that
God is his Father; and this is the beginning of a course of
personal righteousness. Unless and until we know that Jesus
is the Lord and that God is his Father, we do not have testimonies of the truth and divinity of the work. In our day a
testimony is to know, number one, that Jesus is the Lord,
which is the doctrine of the divine sonship. It is to know,
number two, that Joseph Smith is a prophet of God and a
revealer of the knowledge of Christ and of salvation for us
in our day. And it is, number three, to know that The
Church of Jesus Christ of Latter-day Saints is the only true
and living church upon the face of the whole earth. (BYU*
Studies, *Vol. 16, No. 4, pp. 559–60.)*

The Doctrine of Divine Sonship

In order to teach those of our day that we ought to seek after
the same vision of Christ as was known to our ancient fathers,
Nephi tells us that Lehi, his father, received power through his
"faith on the Son of God—and the Son of God was the Messiah
who should come" (1 Nephi 10:17). Following the same pattern, Nephi sought and received the same vision. In that experience these men saw the tree of life. Nephi describes it as having a
beauty and whiteness that exceeded all things. This tree, he was
to learn, was a representation of Christ as the Son of God. (See 1
Nephi 11:4–21.) Developing this same principle, Alma likened
the word of God to a seed, which, he said, if properly cared for

would grow up into a tree, even a tree of life. The fruit of this tree he described as being sweet above all that is sweet, white above all that is white, and pure above all that is pure. The tree from which it comes, the sonship of Christ, Nephi calls the tree of everlasting life. (See Alma 32:28–43; 33:1–23.)

Only if we plant in our hearts the seed of faith in the literal sonship of Christ, as taught by Nephi and Alma, can the full meaning of the grace of Christ and his atoning sacrifice unfold for us. Only if it is understood that God is a personal being, an exalted, glorified man, having body, parts, and passions, can the importance of the birth of Christ be truly understood. If the Father is a personal being and the Son is in his image and likeness, then in the resurrection the Son can become as the Father is. In like manner, only if the resurrection is corporeal, that is, only if body and spirit are inseparably connected, can we too be in the image and likeness of God. Only if this is the case can we hope to retain our individuality in the resurrection. That is, only then can a man expect to be resurrected as a son of God and a woman as a daughter of her divine Father. Only with the preservation of gender in the resurrection can the tender feelings of a man for his wife and a wife for her husband be preserved. The preservation of that love will of necessity bring with it the need to preserve the sanctity of marriage and the family unit. As children of God we will be heirs of God and joint-heirs with Christ. As such we will have claim to the promise of scripture that we might receive of the fulness of the Father, being equal with him in power, might, and dominion. (See D&C 93:19; 76:95.)

Every promise of the gospel, every principle that is sweet to the taste, every doctrine that brings faith and hope, every tenet that lifts and ennobles the soul or that gives purpose to suffering and sorrow, is but an appendage to the doctrine of the sonship of Christ or the fatherhood of God. These principles constitute the true gifts of Christmas. They bring faith, hope, and courage. Nor can it be left unobserved that we find the true worth of such gifts only as we share them with others.

To the witness of those both ancient and modern we add our testimony that Jesus of Nazareth is indeed the Son of God.

References to Gospel Accounts of Christ's Birth

Index